LOOKING FOR THE SAVIOR

A Study of the Thessalonian Epistles • Vol I

DR. DAVID JEREMIAH

with Dr. David Jeremiah

© 2002 by Turning Point for God
P.O. Box 3838
San Diego, CA 92163
All Rights Reserved

Unless otherwise indicated, Scripture verses quoted are taken from the NEW KING JAMES VERSION .

Printed in the United States of America.

Contents

About Dr. David Jeremiah and Turning Point . . 4

About This Study Guide 5

Introduction 7

1. A Dynamic Church
   Acts 17:1–15; I Thessalonians 1:1–10 . . . 9

2. The Marks of a Contagious Christian
   I Thessalonians 1:1–10 23

3. The Gospel According to You
   I Thessalonians 2:1–12 37

4. How to Receive the Word of God
   I Thessalonians 2:13 53

5. The Brotherhood of Suffering
   I Thessalonians 2:14–20 67

6. Growing Up in Your Faith
   I Thessalonians 3:1–13 81

7. The Call to a Holy Life
   I Thessalonians 4:1–12 95

8. The Rapture of the Church
   I Thessalonians 4:13–18 109

Resources 126

Price List 128

About Dr. David Jeremiah and Turning Point

Dr. David Jeremiah is the founder of Turning Point, a ministry committed to providing Christians with sound Bible teaching relevant to today's changing times through radio and television broadcasts, audiocassette series, and books. Dr. Jeremiah's "common-sense" teaching on topics such as family, stress, the New Age, angels, and biblical prophecy forms the foundation of Turning Point.

David and his wife Donna reside in El Cajon, California, where he is the senior pastor of Shadow Mountain Community Church and chancellor of Christian Heritage College. David and Donna have four children and four grandchildren.

In 1982, Dr. Jeremiah brought the same solid teaching to San Diego television that he shares weekly with his congregation. Shortly thereafter, Turning Point expanded its ministry to radio and now television. Dr. Jeremiah's inspiring messages can be heard every day, both nationally and internationally.

Because Dr. Jeremiah desires to know his listening audience, he travels nationwide holding "A Night of Encouragement" ministry rallies and Spiritual Enrichment conferences that touch the hearts and lives of many. According to Dr. Jeremiah, "At some point in time, everyone reaches a turning point, and for every person that moment is unique, an experience to hold onto forever. There's so much changing in today's world that sometimes it's difficult to choose the right path. Turning Point offers people an understanding of God's Word as well as the opportunity to make a difference in their lives."

Dr. Jeremiah has authored numerous books, including *Escape the Coming Night* (Revelation), *The Handwriting on the Wall* (Daniel), *Invasion of Other Gods* (New Age), *Overcoming Loneliness, What the Bible Says About Angels, The Power of Encouragement, Prayer—The Great Adventure, God in You* (Holy Spirit), *Gifts from God* (Parenting), *Jesus' Final Warning, A Bend in the Road,* and *Slaying the Giants in Your Life.*

ABOUT THIS STUDY GUIDE

The purpose of this Turning Point study guide is to reinforce Dr. David Jeremiah's dynamic, in-depth teaching on Thessalonians and to aid the reader in applying biblical truth to his or her daily life. This study guide is designed to be used in conjunction with Dr. Jeremiah's *Thessalonians, Looking for the Savior* audiocassette series, but it may be used by itself for personal or group Bible study.

STRUCTURE OF THE LESSONS

Each lesson is based on one of the tapes in the *Thessalonians, Looking for the Savior* audiocassette series and focuses on specific passages in the Bible. Each lesson is composed of the following elements:

- *Outline*

The outline at the beginning of the lesson gives a clear, concise picture of the passage being studied and provides a helpful framework for readers as they listen to Dr. Jeremiah's teaching.

- *Overview*

The overview summarizes Dr. Jeremiah's teaching on the passage being studied in the lesson. Readers should refer to the biblical passages in their own Bibles as they study the overview.

- *Application*

This section contains a variety of questions designed to help readers dig deeper into the lesson and the Scriptures, and to apply the lesson to their daily lives. For Bible study groups or Sunday school classes, these questions will provide a springboard for group discussion and interaction.

- *Did You Know?*

This section presents a fascinating fact, historical note, or insight that adds a point of interest to the preceding lesson.

USING THIS GUIDE FOR GROUP STUDY

The lessons in this study guide are suitable for Sunday school classes, small-group studies, elective Bible studies, or home Bible study groups. Each person in the group should have his or her own study guide.

When possible, the study guide should be used with the corresponding tape or compact disc series. You may wish to assign the study guide as homework prior to the meeting of the group and then use the meeting time to listen to the message and discuss the lesson.

FOR CONTINUING STUDY

A complete catalog of Dr. Jeremiah's materials for personal and group study is available through Turning Point. To obtain a catalog, additional study guides, or more information about Turning Point, call 1-800-947-1993 or write to: Turning Point, P.O. Box 3838, San Diego, CA 92163.

Dr. Jeremiah's *Turning Point* radio broadcast is currently heard on more than 1150 national and international radio outlets. Contact Turning Point for radio and television program times and stations in your area.

Looking for the Savior

INTRODUCTION

There you were, minding your own business as an average citizen of first century Thessalonica, the largest and most important city in Macedonia. Your town was large and prosperous, and situated on the *Via Egnatia*, the great Roman road that connected Rome with the eastern provinces of the empire. Other north-south trade routes passed through Thessalonica, and its merchants had access to the natural harbor at the head of the Thermaic Gulf. All the traditional Greek cults, religious traditions, and philosophical persuasions were present in your city. Granted, the shadow of Rome was always over your shoulder, but the Emperor kept his distance as long as the citizens stayed in line. Overall, life was good in Thessalonica.

But then one day in A.D. 49 some strangers came to town. Word had it they had been run out of Philippi for preaching some strange new religion. For several weeks they met with Jews in the local synagogue and argued with them about the identity of the Jewish Messiah. Since you had been to the synagogue a number of times you went to listen to what they had to say. And your life was never the same.

For reasons you could not explain, you and a number of other citizens, mostly Gentiles but some Jews, became converts to Christianity. For the first time, in a city filled with religious beliefs, you thought you had heard something you could believe. You embraced the strangers' teachings about Jesus of Nazareth. You asked for, and received, forgiveness for your sins. You, and the other new converts, began to meet together with the strangers—apostles, they were called—to hear more of their teaching when suddenly—they were gone!

The Jews from the synagogue, resentful of the apostles' influence and the defection of Jews to Christianity, got the city officials to make life difficult for the strangers. And to preserve their lives, all of them—Paul, Timothy, and Silas—had to flee the brewing persecutions. And when they did, the brunt of the Jewish and Roman dissatisfaction was brought to bear upon you and your new fellow-believers. You felt like orphans! You were being made to suffer for something you hardly knew how to explain or defend to your accusers. Were you crazy for getting mixed up with this new belief in the first place?

That, or something very close to it, is what occasioned the two letters of Paul to the infant church in Thessalonica. Paul and his companions had been torn away from their new converts, leaving them to face the persecutions and trials being thrust upon them by a hostile religious and civic community. The apostles had had just enough time to teach them the basics of the faith—but not enough time to answer all their questions. Not the least of which were questions about the crucified, but resurrected and ascended, Christ coming back to earth. When? How? And what about some new believers who had already died? Would they miss out on His Second Coming?

In *Looking for the Savior,* Volume 1, we will see what Paul writes in the way of comfort and instruction to a young, persecuted, and insecure group of Christians—and how he commends them for standing up for their new-found Savior in the midst of difficulties. If you know someone in similar circumstances—perhaps yourself?—then you will learn what it takes to advance the faith, stand up for the Gospel, suffer together, live a holy life, and live for the Savior while always looking for His return.

Life was never the same for the new believers in Thessalonica. Indeed, it only got better. As will yours as you study Paul's words to them—and to you.

LESSON 1

A Dynamic Church

Acts 17:1–15; I Thessalonians 1:1–10

In this lesson we unearth the spiritual and historical roots of the church at Thessalonica.

OUTLINE

Many readers think Scripture describes things that were written to inspire but not to be imitated—"We could never be as spiritual as they were back then." Wrong! God gives us a historical portrait of a powerful church so our churches might be just as blessed in spreading the Gospel.

I. **Origin of This Church**
   A. A Dedicated Messenger
   B. A Dynamic Ministry

II. **Operations of This Church**
   A. The Church Had a Converted Membership
   B. The Church Had a Consecrated Ministry
   C. The Church Had a Compassionate Zeal

III. **Opposition to This Church**

IV. **Observations Concerning This Church**
   A. These Are Definite Statements About a Church
   B. This Is a Divine Standard for a Church
   C. These Are the Divine Scriptures About a Church

OVERVIEW

The young church in Thessalonica (ancient Macedonia, modern Greece) was struggling to survive in a dangerous world. Paul wrote his two letters to the church, probably from Corinth, around A.D. 51–52. And within twenty years (A.D. 70) the Roman General Titus stormed through the Middle East and destroyed Jerusalem, killing or taking captive most of the Jews. While far removed from Jerusalem, the church at Thessalonica would have felt the shock waves of Roman oppression of Christianity—waves that were washing upon the shores of the entire Mediterranean region.

I have always liked the Thessalonian letters of Paul because we, like the early Christians, live in dangerous times. In September, 2001, for the first time since Pearl Harbor (1941) American blood was spilled on American soil by foreign enemies. In addition to the military response and economic recession which followed that event, America is facing other dangers as well. Drug and alcohol dependency continue to ruin lives. The AIDS epidemic continues to take lives. Scientists are on the verge of creating a clone of a human being, and living embryos are being used to harvest stem cells for medical research. These and other moral, military, economic, and spiritual crises continue to grow more serious with each new year. And no one is coming forward with answers.

Of course, Christians do not look for answers to today's problems from politicians, educators, or economists. World problems are created by humans who are out of step with God's plan and will, and any solutions for the world we live in will have to originate in the changed hearts of individuals. Only the Gospel of Jesus Christ has answers sufficient for today's dangerous challenges. That is what the Christians at Thessalonica had discovered—and more. The Gospel had changed their lives and was giving them an eternal perspective in spite of what was going on all around them. Though waves of persecution were crashing around them, the believers at Thessalonica were sending forth waves of love and power throughout Macedonia.

As we begin these sixteen lessons covering I and II Thessalonians, let us be motivated and encouraged to have the same impact in our world as the Thessalonians had in theirs.

ORIGIN OF THIS CHURCH

It is important to understand the history of the church at Thessalonica and trace what we know of their spiritual development. There is often a dedicated servant behind the spiritual growth of a new believer, and the same was true for the new body of believers in this Macedonian city.

A Dedicated Messenger

The Apostle Paul was called to Macedonia through a vision in the night: "A man of Macedonia stood and pleaded with him, saying, 'Come over to Macedonia and help us'" (Acts 16:9). Paul concluded the Lord had called him to preach in Macedonia and so went immediately to fulfill that call (Acts 16:10).

Silas and Timothy were with him, and they went first to Philippi where Paul led Lydia to Christ (Acts 16:14), a conversion which marked the founding of the church in Philippi (see Paul's letter to the Philippians). Paul and Silas were arrested and thrown into prison but were miraculously delivered and set free (Acts 16:26), during which time the jailer and his whole family were led to Christ and baptized (Acts 16:30–33).

After encouraging the believers in Philippi a few days, Paul and the rest journeyed to the important city of Thessalonica, a metropolis of 200,000 people. Most of the citizens were Greeks but there were many Romans and Jews there as well. Paul likely went there because it was a center of commerce and other activity. He always went to major cities to establish a basis for evangelism in the region, trusting in new converts to fan out into the surrounding areas after his departure.

According to I Thessalonians 1:5, the message Paul took to the people of Thessalonica was the message of the Gospel: "For our gospel did not come to you in word only, but also in power, and in the Holy Spirit. . . ." In his first letter back to the young church, he reminds them of their foundation: the Gospel of Jesus Christ. It was the Word of God which gave them life and the Word of God which would continue to protect them. The power accompanying the Gospel was not the power of a debater or an orator, but the very power of God. When men see the power of the Holy Spirit at work, their hearts and lives are penetrated and changed. The power of the Spirit is totally different than the power of any man in both impact and effect.

Not only was it powerful, it was persuasive. The Gospel message resulted in "much assurance" for those who believed (verse 5). And it was personalized. The message was backed up and personified in the life of the Apostle Paul: "You know what kind of men we were among you for your sake" (verse 5). The message Paul preached was the same message the Thessalonians saw being lived out before their eyes. An evangelist told me once, "If you preach from your mind, you may change the mind of your hearers. If you preach from your heart, you may change their hearts. But if you preach from your life you will change their lives." The fact that the Holy Spirit had men of integrity through which He could demonstrate His power provided a human link from the Gospel to the Thessalonians.

The Scriptures warn against many becoming teachers since their judgment will be more strict (James 3:1). When we teach the Word of God, and aspire to leadership in the church (I Timothy 3:1 ff.), the message we bring must be validated by our lives. People look to see if we "practice what we preach," if our "walk matches our talk"—and well they should. The most serious thought I have as a preacher of the Gospel is that something I might do in my life would invalidate the message I have preached. My father is an example to me in that regard—a man who preached for more than 60 years without failing in his life to exemplify what he preached. He wasn't perfect, but he was faithful, and the evidence is those his life influenced for Christ.

A Dynamic Ministry

Acts 17 chronicles Paul's ministry in Thessalonica. As was his custom, he went first to the Jewish synagogue and for three Sabbaths "reasoned with them from the Scriptures" (Acts 17:1–2). Paul's method for beginning a ministry where there was no Gospel activity present was to go straight to where the Jews gathered in their synagogue. Not only would he reach Jews with the Gospel, but he would reach the God-fearing Gentiles (Greeks) who gathered with the Jews. Paul knew that the Gospel was "first for the Jew, then for the Gentile" (Romans 1:16 NIV), so he was always faithful to reason with the Jews first. The fact that Paul was in Macedonia instead of Israel was an indication that he was also fulfilling his commission as the apostle to the Gentiles (Romans 11:13).

Luke, the author of Acts, used four words to describe Paul's ministry in the synagogue: reasoning, explaining, demonstrating, and preaching. First, Paul didn't deliver a lecture to his fellow countrymen, the Jews; he reasoned with them, a word which implies discourse based on questions and answers. We could say he dialogued with the Jews, perhaps in the same style that Philip did with the Ethiopian eunuch (Acts 8:30).

Next, Luke says Paul explained the Scriptures. It was customary for someone to read a portion of Scripture and then comment upon it (Luke 4:16–21), so this is likely what Paul did. His goal was to help them see that Christ was the Messiah, the Anointed One spoken of in the Old Testament. Paul evangelized using only the Old Testament!

Then he would demonstrate, which was probably a step beyond explaining. The word demonstrate meant "to lay beside." Paul would pull together a number of passages from the Old Testament and demonstrate the harmony of all of them in pointing to Christ as the Messiah. Paul was trained in the Old Testament, an expert in the law, so his demonstration of the unity of the Scriptures must have been something to behold.

Finally, Luke's last term is preaching, actually quoting Paul himself: "This Jesus whom I preach to you is the Christ" (Acts 17:3). Preaching was the act of proclaiming, Paul's passionate efforts—through reasoning, explaining, and demonstrating—to persuade his listeners to accept Christ. In Paul we see a blending of both teacher and preacher, the reversal of a dichotomy which we have accepted in the modern church without basis. I believe to be a preacher one first has to be a teacher. Preaching is based on the Word of God which has to be studied and organized in a manner that lends itself to presentation and understanding—the task of the teacher. That Word is then proclaimed in a manner that urges the listener to respond. So Paul taught and he preached, moving seamlessly between the two with the Jews and Gentiles in Thessalonica.

Note that the focus of Paul's preaching was scriptural proof concerning Jesus Christ (Acts 17:2–3). He preached a scriptural Christ, a suffering Christ, and a saving Christ. As a result of the clarity of Paul's Gospel presentation, and the movement of the Holy Spirit, many in Thessalonica were saved and became followers of Jesus (verse 4). Paul's methodology is an exhortation to me, and should be to all preachers, to keep our teaching and preaching Scripture-based and Christ-focused. Otherwise, we may succeed in drawing people to our church or to ourselves, but not to Christ.

Scholars are divided over exactly how long Paul stayed in Thessalonica, even though we know it was at least "three Sabbaths" (Acts 17:2). Other evidence suggests it must have been quite a bit longer than that. First Thessalonians 2:7–11 suggests that Paul had gotten a secular job while in Thessalonica so as not to be a material burden on the church. So he was there at least long enough to hold down a temporary job, preaching on a part-time basis. Also, in Philippians 4:16, Paul makes reference to monetary gifts sent to him twice by the Philippian church, while he was in Thessalonica. So he had to be there at least long enough for those gifts to have arrived—and given the overland methods of transportation and delivery of that day, this was probably longer than three weeks.

For however long Paul was there, he carried out a dynamic ministry of preaching and teaching in Thessalonica, winning many to faith in Christ.

OPERATIONS OF THIS CHURCH

The Church Had a Converted Membership

Churches begin for many different reasons, but there was clearly only one reason a church was planted in Thessalonica: Non-Christians were converted to faith in Christ (Acts 17:1–4). In other words, when the church was birthed, its membership consisted of brand new Christian believers. If this strikes you as a mundane observation, it may be because you are unaware of how many churches today have unconverted members. Just because a person is a member of a local church does not mean he or she is a born-again Christian. It should mean that, but it doesn't. People are allowed to join churches, especially in America and Europe where Christianity is part of the historical and social fabric of the nation, without being able to give a clear testimony of faith in Christ. They are "born" into membership, or transfer their membership from another church. Or, they are simply not questioned by the leadership of the church if they have put their personal faith in Christ as Savior and Lord, repented of their sins, and know they have received the gift of salvation leading to eternal life. Unregenerate church members, over time, can act like leaven in a lump of dough—infecting the whole church.

The Church Had a Consecrated Ministry

Paul makes an amazing statement in I Thessalonians 1:3, telling them how he thanked God continually for them—for three specific reasons:

1. Their faith was alive

    We don't often see the words "work" and "faith" in the same context or sentence; they are often viewed as antonyms. But here Paul says the Thessalonians had a "work of faith." In other words, their faith was alive and at work, spreading the Gospel to others and performing words consistent with lives consecrated to Christ. It was a work of faith which produced their conversion, provided their motivation, and promoted their service to end with. Their faith was active and evident for all to see.

2. Their love was active

    In the same verse Paul also says their love was active—a "labor of love," he called it. They worked at their faith and labored at their love. Paul's use of this term is consistent with his description of love in I Corinthians 13. There, Paul pictures love as a series of action words (verbs). And verbs equal labor. Love is costly, requiring the exertion of energy and labor on our behalf toward the object of our love, whether God or man. Several evidences of the labor of their love are found in I Thessalonians 1:6: They followed Paul's example and they followed the Lord, and manifested their love for God with much joy in the Spirit in the face of affliction.

3. Their hope was abundant

    Finally, they had abundant hope (1:3). But not just pointless hope, but hope that was focused on the return of Jesus Christ. It was that hope which gave them patience in the afflictions they were going through. The further we progress in our studies of the two Thessalonian letters, the more we will see how hope permeated the church. They were uniquely focused on the Second Advent of Jesus Christ, and Paul did not want them to be ignorant about His coming.

The Thessalonian believers were known for their faith, love, and hope (I Corinthians 13:13)—but they were also known for their compassionate zeal.

The Church Had a Compassionate Zeal

First Thessalonians 1:8 tells of their zeal to get the Gospel out: "From you the word of the Lord has sounded forth, not only in Macedonia and Achaia, but also in every place. Your faith toward God has gone out, so that we do not need to say anything." This is what happens in a church with a converted membership characterized by faith, hope, and love. Paul was amazed when he discovered the Thessalonian believers had taken the responsibility for evangelizing the surrounding territory. They did not wait for someone else to spread the Gospel around them. They turned from their idols and turned people to God everywhere they could.

Wherever there is that much Gospel activity taking place, there will always be opposition. And the Thessalonians faced their share.

Opposition to This Church

For insight into the opposition to the Gospel in Thessalonica we turn back to Acts 17:5-9. When the Gospel of Christ began to be established in their community, unbelieving Jews did not take it sitting down. They were envious of the success of the apostles and organized a mob from the marketplace to attack the apostles. Going to the house where they were staying, the mob did not find the apostles, but dragged some other believers out of the house and took them before the rulers of the city. The mob accused Jason, the apostles' host, and the other believers, of "acting contrary to the decrees of Caesar, saying there is another king—Jesus" (Acts 17:7). Their intent was to arouse the ire of Rome by accusing the believers of sedition against the Roman emperor.

A general spiritual principle for all Christians to live by is this: When God blesses, there will be opposition. We have had discussions in our church as a staff. As we see God bless various parts of our ministry, we want to be prepared for the opposition we know will arise. A church experiencing the blessing of God is nowhere for spiritual weaklings. The enemy of the church will use any means he can to attack—and often in unsuspected places. I could tell story after story of ways I've seen attacks come in the midst of blessing in the life of our church and its related ministries—even personally and in my family.

Why does this happen? Because when the Gospel makes progress, it is taking light into formerly dark areas. The kingdom of darkness is losing ground and the kingdom of light (kingdom of God) is gaining ground (Colossians 1:13). Lives are changed, wrongs are made right, sin is repented of, forgiveness is extended and received—wonderful things happen when those without Christ find Him. And this displeases the ruler of darkness no end. He wants to keep the world in darkness, so when the light of the Gospel begins to shine in peoples' hearts he will do whatever he can to shut that light off.

When we pray for God to bless us, to enlarge our borders, and to keep His hand upon us in all we do, we must be conscious of praying the last part of Jabez's prayer as well—that God would keep us from evil (I Chronicles 4:9–10). If your borders begin to be enlarged and you start having an impact for Jesus Christ in your circles of influence, prepare for opposition—and pray that God would protect you in it (Matthew 6:13).

A sad commentary on the subject of opposition is that many churches would not know what I am talking about—they are not familiar with the concept of "opposition to the Gospel." Because their church is more of a social outlet for people, and the pastor and leaders serve more as social directors or camp counselors than as heralds of the Word of God, they experience little, if any, opposition. And it is their peaceful existence that gives them the false impression that God is blessing what they're doing.

God's blessing is most evident in churches like the one at Thessalonica where the Gospel is being advanced into pagan territory with measurable results. And with that blessing comes opposition to the message, the messenger, and the ministry.

OBSERVATIONS CONCERNING THIS CHURCH

What can we learn from the experience of the Thessalonians as we begin our in-depth study of Paul's two letters to them? Is it possible for us today to duplicate the kind of spiritual life they had—making an impact on our culture through spreading and living out the Gospel? The answer is "Yes," if we remember three things.

These Are Definite Statements About a Church

First, we are reading history in Acts 17 and in the Thessalonian epistles—not parable, allegory, or story. The church in Thessalonica existed in space and time and was filled with real people who were aflame for the Lord Jesus Christ. Sometimes when we read the Bible we think the things that are recorded in it could only have happened in the Old Testament days or the era of the apostles—that they were more miraculous than things which can happen today. And while that may be true regarding certain periods of miracles, it is not true regarding everyday life in the church. The same Holy Spirit who empowered the church in Thessalonica 1,950 years ago wants to empower the church of the 21st century.

This Is a Divine Standard for a Church

Not only is it possible for the church today to emulate the activities and blessings of the Thessalonian church, it is God's desire that it do so. In other words, being committed and consecrated to Christ, preaching the Word, and spreading the Gospel are not options. Every single local church in our day should be as blessed (and yes, opposed) as the church at Thessalonica.

The Gospel is not to be kept and maintained like a sacred flame burning in a monastery. It is to be taken outside the walls of the church and spread into the darkness that surrounds us. If I have one prayer and plea for the church I pastor as we continue to grow and enjoy God's blessing, it is that we not become an ingrown church, satisfied with where we are. If we are not continually spreading the Gospel further into our community, our nation, and our world, then we are out of God's will for us as a church. These matters are not options, they are a divine standard for the church.

These Are the Divine Scriptures About a Church

Finally, we have been given divine Scriptures about the church at Thessalonica for a reason. And it is not just to learn a history lesson. When we read the divine record, we ought to be convicted about our own lives and the life of our church. If we are not moved to cry out to God, asking Him to do in us what He did in them, we have missed the point of the biblical record. Is there faith, hope, and love in my life? Do I have zeal for spreading the Gospel? Is my life consecrated unto the Lord Jesus Christ?

And most of all, am I part of the converted membership of the church of Jesus Christ? As we begin our study of a great church, I invite you to make sure that the head of the church, Jesus Christ, is also Lord and Savior of your life.

APPLICATION

1. From the following two verses, describe Paul's pre-conversion perspective on Christianity in Jewish synagogues:

    a. Acts 22:19

    b. Acts 26:11

2. After his conversion, where did Paul preach the Gospel first in the following cities:

    a. Antioch of Pisidia (Acts 13:14–15)

    b. Summarize briefly Paul's statement to the Jews (his overall theme): (Acts 13:16–41)

    c. What happened on the following Sabbath? (Acts 13:44)

    d. From what source did opposition arise? (Acts 13:45)

    e. Iconium (Acts 14:1a)

f. The response to their message in Iconium? (Acts 14:1b)

g. The source of opposition in Iconium? (Acts 14:2)

h. Compare the two levels of opposition they received (14:2 and 14:5) and the apostles' response to each (14:3, 6):

i. How would you justify their fleeing the city?

j. Thessalonica (Acts 17:1)

k. Berea (Acts 17:10)

l. The response of the Bereans? (Acts 17:11–12)

m. What is missing from the account regarding Berea?

n. Who supplied the missing opposition? (Acts 17:13)

o. How does Acts 17:13 explain 17:11a?

p. Athens (Acts 17:17)

q. Corinth (Acts 18:4)

r. What response did the synagogue rulers have to Paul's message? (Acts 18:8)

s. Ephesus (second missionary journey) (Acts 18:19)

t. Ephesus (third missionary journey) Acts 19:8)

u. Given the above evidence, how would you describe Paul's evangelistic and apostolic strategy?

3. How would you evaluate Paul's strategy of going to the Jewish synagogues first in every city, in light of his calling as cited in Romans 11:13?

   a. Write a sentence which puts the following pairs of words in their proper order:

   Preaching in synagogues was . . .   The end goal of . . .

   Reaching Gentiles for Christ.   A means to . . .

   b. Fill in the blanks: Paul viewed _____ from the Jews as a measure of his _____ in preaching the Gospel effectively.

4. If opposition is in some ways a measure of success in witnessing, how would you rate your own effectiveness as a witness for Christ?

DID YOU KNOW?

Thessalonica (the modern city is called Salonika) was founded in 316 B.C. by Cassander, an officer of Alexander the Great. It became a seat of Roman administration when Macedonia was made a Roman province in 148 B.C. Because the city has been continually occupied from its founding to the present, there has been little opportunity for archaeological exploration. However, a Roman arch, which stood on the western edge of the city until 1876, bore an inscription making reference to the "politarchs" (city rulers), a previously unknown Greek word. It gave historical credence to Paul's use of the same Greek word in Acts 17:6 to describe the rulers of Thessalonica.

LESSON 2

THE MARKS OF A CONTAGIOUS CHRISTIAN

I Thessalonians 1:1–10

In this lesson we learn what characterizes Christians who impact their culture for Christ.

OUTLINE

Everyone knows of a situation where, instead of the church growing with and changing the community, the community grows without the church's influence. True Christianity is not benign, it is contagious. It infects those who come in contact with it, changing them forever.

I. **Contagious Christians Are Energetic**
   A. Their Energy Comes from an Authentic Conversion
   B. Their Energy Comes from an Aggressive Conduct

II. **Contagious Christians Are Established**

III. **Contagious Christians Are Enthusiastic**

IV. **Contagious Christians Are Evangelistic**

V. **Contagious Christians Are Expectant**

OVERVIEW

One thing we have already learned about the Christians at Thessalonica is that they were a contagious people. Wherever they went they took their faith in Christ and passed it on to others via the Gospel. So much so, Paul said, that there was little else for him to do when it came to following up behind them (I Thessalonians 1:8). The Thessalonians were contagious Christians.

Unfortunately, not all Christians are as positively contagious as were the Thessalonians. Some are more like the Secret Service—you work beside them for five years before you find out they're Christians. And sometimes when you find out they are Christians you wish they weren't—for their faith is in name only. Their lives don't measure up to what they profess to believe. This was definitely not the case with the Thessalonians. They were a group of Christians whom Paul was proud to speak of as models of the faith. They weren't perfect people—no Christians are. But in terms of commitment and zeal for the Lord, and faithfulness in consecrated living, their lives matched their confession.

The Thessalonians discovered at least three things that set them apart: First, they discovered the dynamic of life in Christ. They were genuinely converted by faith in Christ; their lives literally changed. Second, they found the development of life in their church. Their church life was actually a catalyst for spiritual growth; good things happened when they gathered together as a body of believers. Their maturity as believers was evidence of their maturity as a body. And third, they found a discipline which allowed them to live in a culture which was antagonistic to their faith. They lived in a thriving metropolitan area, a seat of Roman influence. But that did not keep them from growing—indeed, it stimulated their growth. No one can grow as a Christian effectively who is not interacting with non-Christians on a regular basis. So their being salt and light in the culture of Thessalonica had a two-way benefit—on the city and on the church.

In light of Paul's enthusiastic commendation of the church at Thessalonica and their impact on their world, we study in this lesson the characteristics of contagious Christians.

CONTAGIOUS CHRISTIANS ARE ENERGETIC

In I Thessalonians 1:3, 9–10 we have evidence of the energy of the Thessalonian Christians. Their work of faith and labor of love and patient hope are all mentioned in verse three, and the fact of their conversion and active anticipation of the return of Christ are mentioned in verses nine and 10. It is plain that their energy in the Christian life came from the authenticity of their conversion.

Their Energy Comes from an Authentic Conversion (9–10)

Words like "saved" and "born again" are used with far too much indiscretion today. Someone has said the "born again" movement is a hundred miles wide and an eighth of an inch deep. While the metaphor probably overstates the case, there is truth in it nonetheless. We have far too many people today claiming to be Christians whose lives don't validate their statements of faith. The Apostle James said that our faith is validated by our works. Faith is the way we are saved, but works should follow. The works of the Thessalonians were clearly evident to Paul: They "turned to God from idols to serve the living and true God" (1:9).

It is important to notice the past tense in that verse—they "turned." Conversion doesn't happen gradually, but rather at a point in time. Just as every person has a time and date of physical birth, so every true Christian has a time and date of spiritual birth. There can be a process leading up to the moment of conversion, but the moment is something that has happened or has not happened. Their Christian faith was evident by what they did following their conversion—they turned from their idols to God. This is the natural pattern for Christians to follow—faith followed by works.

Their idol worship was in the past and their service to God was in the present. But there was also a future aspect of their faith—they were looking for the return of Jesus Christ from heaven (1:10). Their future orientation to life is what energized their present service. They weren't just part of a religion locked out of time and space, drifting aimlessly across the landscape of humanity. They were focused on the fact that a real person, the Lord Jesus Christ, was going to return from heaven to planet earth at some point in the future. Each day, for the Thessalonians, might have been the day Christ would return.

The Thessalonians were energetically contagious because they had been truly converted to Christ. They would never have vacillated or been wishy-washy about what or when they believed. They knew where they stood and in whom they stood, and as a result they were active and energetic in their faith. Energy in living out one's faith is always a benchmark for the genuineness of one's conversion.

Their Energy Comes from an Aggressive Conduct (3)

In our last lesson we noted the work of the Thessalonians' faith, the labor of their love, and the patience of their hope. Their whole lives were characterized by the living out of their faith. They were an active, alive church. They were not like so many churches today which just exist. They don't grow numerically, they don't serve, they don't grow stronger in faith, love, and hope by attempting things which require great faith. They just exist.

Someone said a church is made up of two kinds of people: The pillars who hold it up and the caterpillars who crawl in and out each week. There is probably some truth to that observation. I know I could never be part of a church like that. I am so blessed to be part of a church that is aggressive in living out its faith, that is always looking for ways to do more and be more for Christ and His kingdom. Many in our church are working harder than they sometimes should because they are committed to the prospect that faith is an active enterprise and there are eternal issues at stake—ultimately, the eternal destiny of people.

We will never get it all done and we must be balanced in what we do try to accomplish. But we do want to get to the end of our lives and be able to say that we did everything we knew God asked us to do. If we do that, we will have been contagious Christians just as the Thessalonians were.

CONTAGIOUS CHRISTIANS ARE ESTABLISHED

An important clue about the Thessalonians' stability as Christians is found in verse 5: The Gospel came to them "in much assurance." I think this phrase refers to the confidence Paul and his fellow workers had as they ministered God's truth in Thessalonica. Whether they were in the synagogue or in the street or in someone's home, the Gospel came through them "in power, and in the Holy Spirit" (1:5).

Not only did the preachers preach with assurance, the Thessalonians believed with much assurance. The testimony of faith in the apostles' lives gave the Thessalonians confidence that what they were hearing was truth, and so they believed with confidence. And it was that confidence which established them firmly in their faith as they began to grow and experience the power of the Holy Spirit in their own lives.

And it was apparently the power of the Holy Spirit which gave Paul whatever confidence and authority he possessed as he preached. While we have no biblical descriptions of Paul, traditions from church history have suggested that he was a small, not physically attractive man, who was not even a great speaker. That description seems consistent with some passages in the New Testament regarding Paul and his ministry. For instance, Paul is nowhere described as Apollos was, as an "eloquent man and mighty in the Scriptures" (Acts 18:24). No, it was not Paul's speech or appearance that gave him power. It was his life, empowered by the Holy Spirit.

Paul says that the Thessalonians knew him and his fellow workers, what kind of men they were (1:5). And later in this letter he says that he and his companions had given their very lives for the sake of the Thessalonians' spiritual growth (I Thessalonians 2:8–12). Paul even got a job so he could not be accused of preaching the Gospel in order to get money from his listeners. He worked at his job and ministered to the people in his off hours. When you give your life to people, their lives will change. People will want to know what motivates you to do what you are doing for them. I believe the Thessalonian people wanted what they saw in Paul's life; they wanted to be changed in the same way he had been.

The first two marks of a contagious Christian are that they are energetic and established. Both things were true of the Thessalonian believers and must be true of us as well. You have to be saved and know you're saved, converted and confident of it.

CONTAGIOUS CHRISTIANS ARE ENTHUSIASTIC

It's easy in our modern era of hype and spin to generate a lot of false or ill-founded enthusiasm—something that has no place in the church. We find churches going to great lengths to drum up enthusiasm because they have failed to enter into the God-kind of enthusiasm available to every believer and every church. That enthusiasm is described by Paul in verse six where he mentions "joy of the Holy Spirit."

I just have a feeling that the Thessalonians were an energetic, enthusiastic bunch of Christians. They had received the Word and were enduring affliction together and were a support network for each other. There is something about going through affliction and suffering with others that creates a spiritual synergy resulting in a joy and enthusiasm in spite of the circumstances. Some of the greatest enthusiasm for Christian living I have ever experienced has been in returning to worship at our church after being in the hospital during a period of illness. To come back into the presence of God after an absence and meet with His people creates more enthusiasm in me than anything I know. Being around enthusiastic Christians makes me more enthusiastic as well.

Everyone doesn't express their spiritual enthusiasm the same way, but if we are truly saved we will be excited about the things of God. There will be joy in our lives. The book of Acts is filled with references to the joy experienced and expressed by the early church (Acts 5:41; 8:8; 13:52; 15:3). And so often their joy was expressed in a context of suffering! They counted it a privilege to identify with the sufferings of Christ, and that which was a privilege became a source of joy. No one can be a contagious Christian who walks around with a frown on his face. Who would want to have what they have?

The Thessalonian church had the four key elements required for making an impact on others, all of which are found in verses 5 and 7 of I Thessalonians, Chapter 1. They had the preaching of the Word, the power of the Holy Spirit, assurance, and an impact on others (verse 7). When the Word of God is preached in the power of the Spirit, with the full assurance and conviction that it is true, and that preaching is coupled with a life that measures up to what is preached, then people will be impacted. Lives will be changed. The reason that kind of preaching, and its results, is so noticeable is that there is so little of it taking place today. We have churches and Christians trying everything else except Spirit-filled preaching to generate enthusiasm and life in people. But it will not work.

As I study to prepare messages for our church each week, I get so motivated and impassioned it is hard to contain myself on Sunday morning in the pulpit. It is hard to imagine anyone knowing the truths of the Word of God and not being completely consumed by them on a daily basis. If you recall, there was a period in the life of David when he got away from the Lord due to sin in his life. We have the record of his prayer in Psalm 51 where he prayed, "Restore to me the joy of Your salvation" (verse 12). David wanted the joy back after losing it.

Losing our joy in the spiritual life can have radical consequences on others as well as ourselves. You've probably heard someone say (perhaps you said it before becoming a Christian), "I'd become a Christian if it weren't for so-and-so. He's such a hypocrite." The standard answer to that statement has long been, "Don't look at that person. Instead, look at Jesus. He is not a hypocrite and will never disappoint you." But I want to suggest a different answer— that it does make a difference what people see when they look at us. Why? Because Jesus in you and me is the only Jesus a non-Christian is going to see on this earth. If we are joyless hypocrites in our own lives, don't people have a right to judge our Savior by what they see of Him in us?

In the Bible, leaders never told their followers, "Do what I say, not what I do." In fact, Paul actually told Christians in the churches to imitate him, to practice the Christian life as he practiced it (I Corinthians 4:16; 11:1; Philippians 3:17). Of course, he made sure that he followed Christ so that when the believers followed him they were actually following Christ.

A great verse on the power of an example is I Timothy 4:12— especially for young men in the ministry, or any young person in a position of leadership. Timothy had been put in charge of getting the church at Ephesus in order, yet he was such a young man that his words might not be respected by older believers. So Paul tells him, "Let no one despise your youth, but be an example to the believers in word, in conduct, in love, in spirit, in faith, in purity." Any young person ought to work harder on his life than on his preaching or ministry because it is his life that is going to have the greater impact while he is young. But being a good example is not limited just to the young. Peter tells elders in the church to govern "Not . . . as being lords over those trusted to you, but being examples to the flock" (I Peter 5:3).

Thessalonica was an important city, a crossroads of commerce and ideologies in the ancient world. But rising up out of that secular city was a shining example of Christ living among men, the church of Jesus Christ in Thessalonica. Paul imitated Christ, the Thessalonians imitated Paul, and non-believers imitated the Thessalonians' faith and became Christians. As the church grew, other Christian churches imitated what they heard about in Thessalonica.

They were energetic, established, and enthusiastic—but they were also evangelistic.

CONTAGIOUS CHRISTIANS ARE EVANGELISTIC

In verse 8 we read that the "word of the Lord [had] sounded forth, not only in Macedonia and Achaia, but also in every place." The word "sounded forth" means "to trumpet" or "to blast out" as from a trumpet—a clear, unruffled, undistorted sound. The Gospel came forth from them without shame or embarrassment in clear terms. They had a passion for evangelism.

Is it any wonder the Thessalonians had a passion for evangelism after being around the Apostle Paul? Remember, he was the one who said, "I tell the truth in Christ, I am not lying, my conscience also bearing me witness in the Holy Spirit, that I have great sorrow and continual grief in my heart. For I could wish that I myself were accursed from Christ for my brethren, my countrymen according to the flesh" (Romans 9:1–3). Paul had a passion for reaching people with the Gospel of Christ, and the Thessalonians inherited his passion. They turned out to be just like their teacher when it came to winning souls for Christ!

I want to share something with you that I have shared as a "family" concern with the church I pastor. And that is how the blessing of God is a double-edged sword. There are both positive and negative "benefits" of receiving God's blessing. As our church has prayed for God to bless the various aspects of our ministry over the years, He has answered. I believe our church has been greatly blessed by God. But with that blessing comes a danger. It is possible, slowly over time, to become comfortable and self-satisfied in what we enjoy today in the life of the church. It is possible to lose the vision for reaching those who do not yet know Christ. It is possible to lose the passion for evangelism.

When churches grow and seating and parking and classroom space become a problem, something begins to happen. We stop inviting people to church like we did when the church was smaller and we had plenty of seating, parking, and classroom space. I'm not sure why it happens but I know it does. And we have had to take stock occasionally in the life of our church and ask ourselves, "When was the last time I invited a non-Christian to church or to some sort of evangelistic outreach like a home Bible study group?" We are so busy with our various responsibilities as the church grows that we stop asking, "Who's responsibility is it to reach out to the lost?" And we discover that responsibility isn't getting the attention it used to.

There is nothing like evangelism, and discipling new believers in Christ, to keep any church young and vibrant and passionate about the spiritual life. But if we get so caught up in our activities and responsibilities in ministry to the believers in the church, pretty soon no one is reaching the non-believers. That is the darker side of the blessing of God in church growth. More than anything else in every worship service at our church, I want to know that there are scores of people in our large congregation each week who are hearing the Gospel for the first time. To know that as I preach, empowered by the Holy Spirit, hearts will be opened and lives changed for eternity. But that only happens corporately as the body of Christ continues to reach out in its community to the unsaved.

Reaching the unsaved for Christ is not difficult. It just requires that we never lose our passion for the purpose of the church—to declare the glorious riches of Christ to those who do not possess them, and see those people built into mature believers in Him.

CONTAGIOUS CHRISTIANS ARE EXPECTANT

Verse 10 contains a marvelously clear statement about the priorities and expectations of the Thessalonian church—they were waiting for God's Son to return from heaven to earth. As much as we tend to forget it by getting caught up in the "here and now" of our existence, there is an undeniable urgency bound up in the Gospel message. Christians believe that Christ is going to return to earth one day to consummate history. All who die in their sins before that event occurs will spend a Christless eternity apart from heaven. If that is not a motivation for evangelism, I don't know what is. The Thessalonians believed that truth and were motivated by it to reach those who lived around them.

I often ask our church, "If you knew Jesus Christ was going to return tonight so that tomorrow there would be no more opportunity to be saved, who would you go home and call on the phone? What would happen to your fear of witnessing? How would your priorities be changed?" I have a feeling a lot of unsaved people would find their phone ringing and hear knocks on their door, being contacted by Christians concerned that they not miss their last opportunity to be saved. But the truth is, Jesus could come back tonight. He could appear in the heavens at any moment. Yet we have not let that fact keep us living on the edge of expectancy in reaching others for Christ.

The word "wait" means a patient, steadfast alertness toward the return of the Lord Jesus. It wasn't a passive waiting; it was an active waiting. It was the kind of waiting that controlled their lives. That for which they waited was going to have global implications, and they knew it. Therefore they lived their lives in light of the implications of that event. I fear the church has allowed the light of the return of Christ to grow dim in the modern era. Preachers rarely preach on the topic from their pulpits since it is an "either-or" message. Either you are saved and will welcome His return or you are not and you will run to hide yourself at His return.

The Thessalonian Christians expected Christ's return, and joyfully so. My prayer is that, as we study further in these letters, you will find yourself identifying with them; that their contagious faith will infect you thoroughly and everyone with whom you come in contact. True Christianity is contagious Christianity. May it spread far and wide!

APPLICATION

1. Read Matthew 5:13–16.

    a. Besides flavoring, what was the use of salt in the ancient world Jesus is referring to? (verse 13)

    b. In what way are Christians to function as salt in an antagonistic culture?

    c. How do you reconcile Jesus' command to be a preservative in a world that is destined to be destroyed?

    d. What is the chief purpose of light? (verse 15)

    e. What does Jesus suggest needs illuminating in our world? (verse 16)

    f. How would you compare I Thessalonians 1:3 with Jesus' command to be light in the world?

    g. What are the main "works of faith" and "labors of love" that are available to you which would illuminate Christ in your part of the world?

h. How effective are you at being salt and light? How effective would you say the Thessalonians were?

2. Read James 2:14–26.

   a. What is the central thesis of this section? (verse 14)

   b. How should your deeds differ between a person who has legitimate needs and one whose needs result from a wanton or profligate lifestyle? (verses 15–16)

   c. What do works prove about faith? (verse 17)

   d. What is the meaning of verse 24, theologically speaking?

   e. In light of verse 26, would you say the Thessalonians' faith was alive or dead? (I Thessalonians 1:3)

3. Read II Corinthians 6:3–10.

   a. Why was Paul a qualified spokesman for living "energetically" for Christ?

b. What are the major hindrances to Christians following Paul's example today? (Read through the list again in light of the average American family with several children, two jobs, etc.)

c. Paul obviously deprived himself of a great deal. How do you personally find the balance between living energetically for Christ versus living energetically for yourself?

d. Identify all the things in these verses which every Christian could do (e.g., verse 6):

e. If someone who knew you well before you were a Christian met you now, how energetic would they say you are as a Christian?

f. The Thessalonians turned from idols to serve the true God. What distinct changes in your life indicate an authentic conversion?

4. When is it wise to imitate other Christians? (I Corinthians 11:1)

a. How will you know whether a Christian leader is following Christ or not?

b. Under what conditions would you urge a fellow believer to imitate you? (I Corinthians 4:16)

c. In what practical ways was Paul a model to the Thessalonian church? (II Thessalonians 3:7–10)

5. Read Acts 5:41; 8:8; 13:52; 15:3.

   a. In how many instances was the church's joy related to the advancement of the Gospel?

   b. How often is that the cause of joy in the modern church?

DID YOU KNOW?

Oscar Cullmann, the European theologian, has pointed out that every major military campaign in history has had a battle which was the turning point of the war. Napoleon met his final defeat at Waterloo in 1815. The Confederate states' fate was sealed with the Union victory at Gettysburg in 1863. And the turning point of World War II occurred with the Allied invasion of Europe on the beaches of Normandy in 1944. Similarly, in the spiritual war of good versus evil, the three-day death and resurrection of Christ insured that He and His followers are victors. Though spiritual skirmishes still occur, the fate of our enemy is sealed. We live expectantly and confidently, awaiting the return of our victorious King.

LESSON 3

THE GOSPEL ACCORDING TO YOU

I Thessalonians 2:1–12

In this lesson we are given six pictures of a faithful minister of the Gospel.

OUTLINE

If you were asked to list six words describing an effective minister of the Gospel, you might get one or two of the ones Paul cites. But his list is forged from the crucible of experience. Paul knew what it took to be effective—and you will too after studying his words.

I. We Must Be Courageous as Good Soldiers

II. We Must Be Conscientious as Stewards
  A. The Gospel Must Be Presented Courageously
  B. The Gospel Must Be Presented Clearly
  C. The Gospel Must Be Proclaimed Convincingly

III. We Must Be Cautious as Gracious Servants

IV. We Must Be Comforting as a Godly Mother

V. We Must Be Careful as a Godly Example
  A. Careful to Minister from a Clear Heart
  B. Careful to Maintain a Clear Conscience
  C. Careful to Manifest a Consistent Life

VI. We Must Be Concerned as a Father
  A. A Father Challenges When It Is Needed
  B. A Father Comforts When It Is Needed
  C. A Father Charges When It Is Needed

OVERVIEW

The Thessalonians were contagious Christians (see the last lesson) because of the manner in which they went about serving the Lord. In the first 12 verses of I Thessalonians 1, we have six pictures of a servant of God who carries out effective ministry. These pictures are primarily of the Apostle Paul and his fellow workers in the Gospel. But there is no doubt the Thessalonian Christians learned how to serve the Lord from Paul (II Thessalonians 3:7-10), so his example serves as an example to us as we study the Thessalonian church.

Paul begins chapter two of I Thessalonians in an interesting fashion—by mentioning nine negatives in verses 1 through 6. These constitute ways *not* to do the work of the ministry: not in vain, from error, uncleanness, deceit, pleasing men, using flattering words, with covetousness, seeking glory from men, seeking glory from the Thessalonians or others. That is an interesting grid through which every Christian could look at his own service for Christ. If we serve the Lord with any of those attitudes or perspectives, we are not doing the work of the ministry as we should.

Then, in verses seven through 12 Paul mentions positive things that should characterize the ministry: gentleness, imparting the Gospel, imparting our own lives, preaching the Gospel of God, exhorting, comforting, and charging one another.

In this lesson we will combine Paul's lists into a study of six kinds of people we ought to be as we serve the Lord: good soldiers, stewards, gracious servants, godly "mothers," godly examples, and fathers. Paul was all of these to the Thessalonians and they learned to become these by following his example—as can we.

WE MUST BE COURAGEOUS AS GOOD SOLDIERS (2:1-2)

Paul begins by recounting to the Thessalonians how he came to them after suffering greatly at Philippi (Acts 16). Even after having been beaten and thrown into jail in Philippi, Paul still was not discouraged. After his miraculous release, he left Philippi and went straight into Thessalonica and began to preach boldly again as if nothing had happened. Nothing could induce Paul to tone down his message to make it less offensive or more seeker-friendly. That is not true of many modern preachers who preach everything except the Gospel from their pulpits. They never preach about the blood of Christ, the cross, hell, judgment, or the return of Christ. They consider those topics too controversial. It is hard to say why a truly converted preacher would not want to preach on all the counsel of God—and especially the Gospel.

Paul was a man not afraid to preach the truth. As soldiers of the cross, we must have the same boldness that a soldier in wartime must have. How much chance is there of winning a war if the soldiers are not bold? It is the Gospel which is the power of God unto salvation, and the Gospel which must be the centerpiece of our preaching. Even in times of "much conflict" we must not hold back. Even though he had been beaten with "many stripes" and put in stocks in Philippi (Acts 16:23–24), Paul preached to the very next person with whom he came in contact—the Philippian jailer—and won him to Christ.

Paul was bold in jail and out of jail. In jail, he and Silas sang hymns to God in the middle of the night before they were released by God's intervention. Then once they were out, and the officers realized they had beaten a Roman citizen without a hearing, Paul was again bold. He made the officers own up to what they had done before he would leave peaceably. Paul feared no man, civil or religious. He took his boldness in God into every arena of his life.

WE MUST BE CONSCIENTIOUS AS STEWARDS (2:3–5)

In verse 4 Paul says he had been approved by God "to be entrusted with the gospel." This is a remarkable truth, not only for Paul but for us as well. The Gospel has been given to us as a sacred stewardship for which we are responsible. It was given first by God and was bequeathed to us by the prior generation for safekeeping and responsible stewardship. How thankful we should be that those who have gone before have left us the complete Gospel—not a watered down version which has no power. Unfortunately, many churches pass on an anemic message from one generation to the next—a gospel that cannot save.

Many times in Scripture the message and words of God are pictured as a divine trust, something deposited in the inner man, a divine spark which must be nurtured and preserved. The command to preach was given to Paul (Titus 1:3); the Gospel was given to him as a trust (I Timothy 1:11–12); even the terror of the Lord in judgment was something he was in awe of (II Corinthians 5:11). Even Jeremiah held the Word of God in himself as a "burning fire shut up in [his] bones" (Jeremiah 20:9)—a fire he could not contain.

The Gospel Must Be Presented Courageously

In many ways, I think of my own father when I think of the Apostle Paul. For more than sixty years he proclaimed the Gospel boldly wherever he went. I can remember as a young boy growing up, my father would always witness to the gas station attendant who pumped gas into the car (that was before the days of self-serve gas stations). Of course, I was highly embarrassed at his boldness—which is more a reflection on me than him. I didn't see why he had to witness to everyone wherever we went. He would convey the Gospel message while the gas was being pumped, and always leave a Gospel tract. That kind of witnessing used to be quite common, but we rarely see it anymore. We are more concerned about not offending someone than we are about the lost state of his soul. But Paul was not concerned with any offense except the offense of the cross (Galatians 5:11).

The Gospel Must Be Presented Clearly

Courage without clarity results in confusion. Therefore the Gospel must be presented in such a way that it is receivable by the intended audience. This is Paul's point in verses 3 and 5: We didn't use error, uncleanness, deceit, flattery, or covetousness in presenting the Gospel. In other words, Paul had no ulterior motives. He presented the Gospel simply and sincerely.

1. Our motive should be simple

    Flattery is not sincere. In fact, it is the opposite—as insincere a form of communication as can be imagined. Flattery means saying something in order to get something from the person you are flattering. Someone has said flattery does not communicate, it manipulates. Paul did not lower himself to use flattering words in order to get his listeners to hear and believe the Gospel. He did not use buttery speech or sweet-sounding words in order to win the approval of his hearers. He simply preached the Gospel in all its awesome simplicity, allowing it to speak for itself as empowered by the Holy Spirit.

    I wish we could say today that preachers were more concerned about conveying the Gospel simply and powerfully than they are about filling the pews in their church. But there is a mentality abroad that says, first and foremost, we must draw a crowd. And to do that we will say whatever will not turn people away. Don't misunderstand—it's not my goal to drive people away from the church. I love as much as anyone the thought that someone has been encouraged and built up by my sermons. But if you go away encouraged with a smile on your face, but lost because you didn't hear the Gospel, then I have a problem. I don't want my doctor to flatter me by telling me how good everything looks except for the tumor I have. I want to hear the truth from the only one who can give it to me plain and simple.

William Barclay, in his commentary on I Thessalonians, cited a passage from *The Didache*. This was a handbook on church matters written somewhere between the first and third centuries. In it, the author warns against the motives and behavior of false apostles. They over-extend their stay in homes; they ask for money; they take extra food with them when they leave. These were signs that something was amiss. Neither apostles nor their message was to be complicated or self-indulgent or flattering. Since apostles had no ulterior motives, they had no reason to ingratiate themselves to others.

2. Our motive should be sincere

Paul says, "God is [my] witness" (2:5). He did not hesitate to call God into the room to validate who he was and what he was proclaiming and what his motives were in all of it. Paul did not enter Thessalonica, or any other city, hiding behind a cloak of covetousness. There was nothing that he saw that the people owned that he was trying to get from them. His motives were pure and sincere in all that he did.

The Gospel Must Be Proclaimed Convincingly

In verse four, Paul says he came to Thessalonica speaking not to please men but to please God. At no time did Paul accommodate himself to the desires of men in his preaching (Galatians 1:10; 2:11–14).

Preachers who try to accommodate their message to the desires of their audience are in danger of diluting and distorting the Gospel. It is important for us to have our finger on the pulse of the culture and know what people are thinking and going through. And it is doubly important for us to address the

Gospel to those needs. But the one thing we must never do is accommodate the message to those needs—that is, change the message so it says something it doesn't really say. It's one thing to make people feel better while staying in their condition, and another altogether to present a truth that will get them out of their condition. The former is accommodating ourselves to their need, the latter is meeting their need.

God, not people or the culture, is the one who tests all of our ministry done in His name. The text of verse 4 says He "keeps on testing and approving our hearts." It is only to Him that we owe allegiance since it is His judgment before which we shall one day stand (Romans 14:12; I Corinthians 4:5).

WE MUST BE CAUTIOUS AS GRACIOUS SERVANTS (2:6)

Verse 6 reveals that Paul had the heart of a servant. He was an apostle to be sure, but he came seeking no glory nor making demands from the Thessalonians.

It's hard to imagine the Apostle Paul ever losing sleep over what other people thought of him. That does not mean he was arrogant. Quite the contrary. He was constantly conscious of how his life reflected on the Lord Jesus Christ. But he was not self-aware or self-serving. Like any good servant, his desire was to decrease so that Jesus might increase (John 3:30). His goal in life was simply to serve the Lord "with all humility" (Acts 20:19). When he preached, his goal was to preach Christ, not himself (II Corinthians 4:5). A true servant has only one desire—to do his master's bidding. And that was Paul's aim throughout his apostleship.

WE MUST BE COMFORTING AS A GODLY MOTHER (2:7–8)

In verses 7 and 8 Paul takes on the role of a strikingly different character—that of a nursing mother. His words are so tender and affectionate that they deserve our reading: "But we were gentle among you, just as a nursing mother cherishes her own children. So, affectionately longing for you, we were well pleased to impart to you not only the gospel of God, but also our own lives, because you had become dear to us."

Sometimes being a minister to others is like being a mother. When a child is born the mother is on call 24 hours a day. At any time she may be called upon to meet her baby's needs. While it is taxing, even exhausting work, the mother does not mind because she is nurturing new life which she has brought into the world. And when that child reaches the age at which he leaves home, that mother never tires of seeing his figure in the doorway, always longing and watching for his return. And no matter how old he gets, she never ceases to be his mother. How is his health? Who are his friends? Is he eating and sleeping well? Is he happy in what he is doing? It is impossible to get a child out of a mother's heart.

Paul uses that mother as the illustration of how he felt about the Thessalonians—and how we all are to minister to one another in the family of God. Those whose spiritual birth we are responsible for, or whose early stages of growth we witness, will forever be in our hearts as a child is in a mother's heart. Paul cared for his converts, not with harsh admonitions, but with the loving and gentle touch of a tender mother. In the same way, we are to feel empathetically toward young believers; we are to feed them with the nourishment of the Word of God; and we are to fortify their souls with words of encouragement and sound doctrine. We are to do it all tenderly.

Men in ministry need to learn the lessons of tenderness from their mothers and wives. There is nothing wrong with being tender as an apostle, a pastor, a teacher, or a leader. Paul himself said in II Timothy 2:24 that the "servant of the Lord must not quarrel, but be gentle to all, able to teach, patient." Paul identified another aspect of ministering like a mother in II Corinthians 12:15: Babies and children don't always love back. He said, "the more abundantly I love you, the less I am loved." Mothers don't love in order to be loved in return, nor should those who minister.

WE MUST BE CAREFUL AS A GODLY EXAMPLE (2:9–10)

Not only is the attitude we have in ministry important, but the example we set for others as well. In verse 10 Paul says, "You are witnesses, and God also, how devoutly and justly and blamelessly we behaved ourselves among you who believe." There is no other way to say some things than the plain way: If you are going to be used by God you will have to walk to the beat of a different drum. Your standards must be higher, your walk closer, and your path straighter. Why? Because you must be an example to those you lead.

Careful to Minister from a Clear Heart

Paul says that he and his co-laborers worked devoutly among the Thessalonians. His heart was not divided between his work for God as an apostle and his work for himself. His heart was pure insofar as his motives and actions were concerned.

Careful to Maintain a Clear Conscience

In Acts 24:16 Paul confesses to a clear conscience being a high priority in his life—with regard to both God and man. A Christian with a clear conscience is a powerful tool in the hand of God. A person who is free to act, free to respond to whatever direction God gives, is truly a free person. But when there is something you feel guilty about, and you constantly wonder who else knows about it, there is a ball and chain attached to your soul. You are not a free person. It is a liberating thought to know that no one could come forward to accuse you of anything you have hidden or tried to cover up—because your conscience is clear.

Careful to Manifest a Consistent Life

One of the most awesome realities I live with daily is the fact that I could undo in a moment what God has developed in my life over the last 20 years. One act of rebellion against God is all it would take. An unguarded moment in the presence of temptation has brought down the ministry of more than one man of God in our day. It is the greatest fear of my life, and one I pray daily will never come to pass. I would rather God take me off this earth than allow me to bring reproach upon His name and destroy what influence I have had for the Gospel with an act of sin. Maintaining a consistent life, a life of accountability and holiness, is a requirement for one who ministers to others. We have already noted that it was the consistency of the life of Paul, and his fellow workers, that gave him such authority before people (I Thessalonians 1:5). The minister who does not guard his life, who does not realize that life is lived on the edge of a cliff, is a minister who is ready to succumb to the snares of this world.

Don't be mistaken—the issue is not perfection. If it were, then none of us could stand; none of us could minister. The issue is a clear heart, a clear conscience, and a consistent life. Every minister of the Gospel will fail in some points, at some time. But the minister who does will be on his knees immediately restoring his walk with the Lord and asking for renewed strength and grace to carry on afresh.

WE MUST BE CONCERNED AS A FATHER (2:11-12)

The final picture Paul gives of the effective minister for Christ is that of a father: "As you know how we exhorted, and comforted, and charged every one of you, as a father does his own children, that you would walk worthy of God who calls you into His own kingdom and glory" (2:11-12).

It is interesting that Paul includes both the tender mother and the exhorting father in the same chapter of Scripture, and sees himself in both roles in the lives of the Thessalonians. I remember a pattern in my home growing up that I imagine has been true in many besides my own. That is, if I would misbehave in some way during the day my mother would say, "Your father will deal with this when he gets home!" Not only would I have to live with a sense of dread the rest of the day, but I had to experience whatever level of displeasure my actions provoked from my father. I can still recall the sound, and remember the site, of his car coming in the driveway as I knew I was about to be "dealt with."

There are times for tenderness and times for sternness in each of our lives—and Paul was equipped to handle both roles as an apostle.

A Father Challenges When It Is Needed

"Exhortation" means to call to one's side; to draw alongside someone and urge them toward a course of action. It is what I do with my children, even as they get older and establish marriages and families of their own. They aren't required to follow my advice, of course, but I still feel a fatherly responsibility to exhort and encourage them as a friend. Whether they take my advice is up to them, but it is part of the father's role to give it out of love and concern.

A Father Comforts When It Is Needed

Sometimes it is not advice that is needed, but comfort. At times a child, or a young Christian, just needs to know that a fatherly figure understands what they are going through. One of my sons recently was a witness to a grinding automobile accident near his college campus; actually witnessed a man perish in a flaming wreck. That was the worst thing he had ever seen in his young life, and he was shaken. My job at that point was simply to try to comfort him, to encourage him, to walk through his memory of that terrible experience. Comfort may be intuitively more of a mother's role, but it is a father's responsibility as well.

A Father Charges When It Is Needed

Finally, a father charges those under his care. A "charge" is an urging, a strong exhortation, but one that is based on personal experience. And the emphasis is on those who are more mature ministering to those who are less mature—just as a father does his children. Just as a father tells his children about how life was when he was a boy, so a father-minister tells his young charges about his experiences as a believer—how the Lord saw him through difficult experiences. Having gone through cancer treatment myself, I find I can now minister effectively to others who are facing that same ordeal. My experience gives me the ability to play a "fatherly" role in their lives.

The goal of all six of the portraits Paul presents in these verses is found in verse 12: "that you would walk worthy of God who calls you into His own kingdom and glory." That's what Paul wanted for the Thessalonians, and it is what he would want for us as well. Likewise, it is what we should want for every person we minister to. It is an awesome privilege to be a minister of the Gospel for the glory of God.

APPLICATION

1. Read Philippians 1:27–30.

    a. What happened in Philippi to which Paul is making reference here? (Acts 16:16–24)

    b. In the face of such opposition, what special meaning does Paul's exhortation in verse 27 have?

    c. What is worthy conduct in the face of opposition to the Gospel?

    d. What would be considered unworthy conduct?

    e. Why is maintaining "one spirit" and "one mind" important for the church when facing opposition?

f. Why are one's adversaries a proof of salvation? (verse 28)

g. What is granted to every believer in Christ? (verse 29)

h. In what additional way did Paul expect the churches to imitate him? (verse 30)

i. What did Paul do after suffering in Philippi? (Acts 16:40–17:1) Did he view suffering as a normal or abnormal part of his responsibility as a Christian apostle?

j. What is the greatest degree of suffering you have experienced that was directly attributable to being a Christian?

2. From the following verses, identify various aspects of Paul's life as a good soldier for Christ:

   a. What does the word "labor" add to your understanding of Paul's life? (Colossians 1:29)

   b. What is the word in this verse which contributes to the "soldier" metaphor? (Colossians 2:1)

   c. What preceded Paul's boldness in Thessalonica? (I Thessalonians 2:2)

   d. What did Paul do to "take hold of the eternal life" to which he was called? (I Timothy 6:12 NIV)

e. To what does he equate keeping the faith? (II Timothy 4:7)

f. Even without active persecution by non-Christians, in what other ways is the modern Christian life a "struggle" similar to soldiering?

g. How does the idea of a "struggle" contrast with modern emphases on convenience and comfort?

h. How is the spiritual experience weakened by a failure to engage in "fighting the good fight?"

3. Read I Corinthians 15:1–11.

   a. What is Paul discussing in this passage? (verse 1)

b. What does the Gospel accomplish in the one who believes it? (verse 2)

c. What are the "non-negotiables" of the Christian Gospel? (verses 3–4)

Christ _____, was _____, and _____ again.

d. How much of that Gospel did Paul preach? (verse 11)

e. What must any steward of the Gospel declare in order to be faithful?

f. What would you say about a church that called itself Christian but did not preach the death, burial, and resurrection of Christ—and the meaning of each?

4. Before whom did Paul constantly strive to maintain a clear conscience? (Acts 24:16)

   a. Over time, how can your conscience become attuned to the things of God? (Romans 9:1)

   b. What does a clear conscience give one the power to do? (II Corinthians 1:12)

   c. What effect does a clear conscience have on any who would accuse you wrongly? (I Peter 3:16)

DID YOU KNOW?

The word which Paul uses in I Thessalonians 2:3 for deceit is *dolos*. This was the word originally used for bait that was used to catch fish or an animal. In its very nature, bait is something that pretends to be the real thing, but is not. It is the appearance of reality which lures the innocent prey into destruction. For Paul to have been a *dolos* himself, he would have had to have been a false apostle—one that looked like an apostle on the outside but was not in reality. There were false apostles in Paul's day; indeed, he encountered their deceit more than once. Fortunately, God gave Paul the signs of a true apostle which verified who he really was (II Corinthians 11:13–15; 12:12).

LESSON 4

How to Receive the Word of God

I Thessalonians 2:13

In this lesson we discover how the Word of God produces dynamic Christian faith.

OUTLINE

Every church wants to change the world, to make a difference. But the myriad ways churches go about reaching that goal suggest they really don't know how to do it. A church in the first century changed its world by believing one simple truth: The Word of God is God's words to us.

I. Accepting the Word of God

II. Acknowledging the Word of God

III. Anticipating the Word of God

IV. Appreciating the Word of God

V. Applying the Word of God
 A. The Word of God Converts Your Soul
 B. The Word of God Cleanses Your Life
 C. The Word of God Will Control Your Walk
 D. The Word of God Causes You to Grow
 E. The Word of God Counsels Your Decisions
 F. The Word of God Confirms Your Salvation

OVERVIEW

We are learning that the church of Thessalonica was a dynamic church, one willing to stand together against opposition and boldly proclaim the Gospel in surrounding territories. So effective were they that Paul said there was little he could add to their testimony when he visited places they had already been (I Thessalonians 1:8).

What makes a church like that stand out? What was their secret? And more importantly, why don't we have more churches like the Thessalonian church today? We know that suffering, in a paradoxical way, empowers a church. And we will see in our next lesson that the Thessalonian church suffered for their faith (Acts 17:5–9). But does that mean a church that is not persecuted cannot be dynamic? No—there must be additional factors. And I believe we see the core of their vibrancy in one verse: "For this reason we also thank God without ceasing, because when you received the word of God which you heard from us, you welcomed it not as the word of men, but as it is in truth, the word of God, which also effectively works in you who believe" (I Thessalonians 2:13).

I believe the Thessalonians had a perspective on the Word of God which informed everything they did. It was not just words to them—it was something to be received, welcomed, and internalized that it might do its work in them. The life they lived externally was a direct reflection of the Word of God they internalized. Our understanding of how they responded to the Word of God will go a long way toward our becoming the kind of dynamic Christians they were individually and corporately.

ACCEPTING THE WORD OF GOD

The Word of God Paul refers to in verse 13 is that which he preached to the Thessalonians when he evangelized them. Romans 10:17 says that "faith comes by hearing and hearing by the Word of God." They heard the Word and faith followed. Since there is a continual need for faith to "come" even after we are saved, we must ask, "How do we continue to receive the Word of God?"

Hopefully the main source for all Christians is through a diligent and consistent study of the Bible. We have what the Thessalonians didn't have—our own copy of the words God has given to mankind. But we also receive the Word of God through regular attention to it being preached. We attend a local church and (hopefully) hear the Bible faithfully preached, the Gospel faithfully proclaimed. Paul says it is by the foolishness of preaching that men are saved, so we continue to preach (I Corinthians 1:21–25 KJV). We also receive the Word through Sunday school classes and Bible study groups. Television, radio, VHS and cassette tapes—there are so many mediums by which we can accept the Word of God into our lives. I discovered recently that you can listen to the entire Bible on audio cassette tapes in 72 hours. The average person spends that much time watching television in a few weeks time. So if one simply cut out television for a while he could receive the entire Word of God in the same time period.

In spite of all these ways to receive the Word of God, the ancient words of the prophet Amos apply to us today: There is a famine in the land, not of bread or water, "but of hearing the words of the Lord" (Amos 8:11). There is in our culture today a famine of hearing the words of the Lord. Past generations used to hear the word of the Lord all across our land regardless of the denomination. It was present in schools, and even in the government. But that is not true today.

It is possible to hear the Word of God physically but not spiritually; externally but not internally. Jesus taught this Himself when He explained His use of parables (Matthew 13:13). And James reminds us that we have been called not to be hearers only of the Word, but doers as well (James 1:22). So we have to guard against the deception of thinking that because we attend church or a Bible study that the Word is really changing our lives. But hearing and receiving the Word is indeed the first step. Without that nothing will happen.

ACKNOWLEDGING THE WORD OF GOD

Receiving the Word of God is more than just hearing it. It is accepting and acknowledging that it is the Word of God for you. You're hearing words which are different from the words in your newspaper or television newscast. You are hearing words which have come from God. You are really hearing the Word when you agree with Job who said, "I have treasured the words of His mouth more than my necessary food" (Job 23:12).

Throughout Scripture, those who received the Word of God placed the highest value on it. Most frequently it was said to be more valuable than gold, silver, or treasures (Psalm 119:14, 72, 127, 162). David also said that, for him, the Word of God was even more valuable than sleep (Psalm 119:148). How many times have you awakened at night and turned to the Word of God just to savor its truth in the middle of the night? Most of us are so tired at night we don't wake up for anything. But try it next time that happens to you—see if the Word of God doesn't have even more value than sleep.

There are many ways we can acknowledge the place of the Word of God in our lives. But if it is genuinely precious to us, it will show—one way or another.

Anticipating the Word of God

The word "welcomed" which Paul uses to describe the Thessalonians carries with it the sense of expectation. They anticipated hearing the Word of God; they wanted to hear it; they looked forward to hearing it. This is yet another way to determine whether a person is hearing the Word of God with the inner ears or with the outer ears only. Do you look forward to hearing the teaching and preaching of the Word? Do you look forward to your own discovery of the riches of the Word in Bible study?

It's not unusual for me to encounter born-again Christian people who resist the Word of God. They've almost become jaded or cynical about it the older they are in the faith. They have built a wall of defense, not wanting the Word to have access to their hearts and lives. People get set in their ways and don't want to be challenged. But should a true Christian not always welcome whatever the God of the universe has to say, fresh each day? I believe a person's attitude toward the Word of God is a barometer of sorts about their whole spiritual life. Specifically, our response to the Word is indicative of our response to Christ Himself. They are both the Word of God. The Bible is the written Word of God and Jesus Christ is the living Word of God. How could our response to one be different from our response to the other? Look at the ways in which they are similar:

> 1. They are both bread. Jesus Christ said in John 6:48, "I am the bread of life." But He also reminded the devil that the words of God are bread as well: "Man shall not live by bread alone, but by every word that proceeds from the mouth of God" (Matthew 4:4). So both the written and living Word of God are bread for life.
>
> 2. They are both light. "Then Jesus spoke to them again, saying, 'I am the light of the world. He who follows Me shall not walk in darkness, but have the light of life'" (John 8:12). But the written Word is light, too. Psalm 119:105 says, "Your

word is a lamp to my feet and a light to my path." Both the written Word and the living Word are light.

3. They are both truth. "Jesus said to him, 'I am the way, the truth, and the life. No one comes to the Father except through Me'" (John 14:6). Jesus also said that the Word of God was truth: "Sanctify them by Your truth. Your word is truth" (John 17:17). So once again, the living Word is truth and the written Word is truth.

In all three of these cases, we are not likely to honor one form of bread, light, or truth over the other. How we approach the written Word of God is probably a good indication of how we approach the living Word. Therefore, it is impossible for someone to say they have a great relationship with Christ, but they never read the Bible: "I'm all about Jesus, but I just don't get into studying." Since the Bible, from cover to cover, is all about Jesus Christ, it's difficult to imagine how someone could be interested in Jesus without being interested in the Word.

So, these believers from Thessalonica not only heard the Word of God and received the Word of God, they welcomed and anticipated the Word of God. The Word of God to them was the message of Almighty God concerning Jesus Christ His Son.

APPRECIATING THE WORD OF GOD

The key to appreciating the Word of God is to receive it and welcome it "not as the word of men, but as it is in truth, the word of God" (I Thessalonians 2:13). This statement by Paul is one of the surest affirmations we have that the apostles considered their teachings to be the Word of God. When Paul preached the Gospel to the Thessalonians, they were hearing the Word of God. Not from the top of Sinai, or from the midst of the tabernacle, but on a street corner, in a synagogue, or in a home in downtown Thessalonica. The Word of God traveled with, and was proclaimed by, the apostles of God. Paul would have been heartbroken if they had received his words as the "word of Paul" instead of the Word of God. He gave unceasing thanks to God that this was not the case (verse 13).

In our pluralistic and politically correct culture, the Bible is now regarded as the word of man. Courses are taught on the Bible as literature and as a sourcebook for ancient history or for comparative religious studies. The Bible is great literature, history, and theology—but those three disciplines never saved anyone for eternity or changed their life in time. Only God's Word can do that. Some take the middle ground, saying the Bible "contains" God's Word, but is not God's Word itself. That is, some parts are inspired and some are not. But who, may I ask, is the arbiter and judge who can tell us which parts are God's words and which parts are man's words? The Bible stands or falls as a unit. Either it is all the Word of God or none of it is.

Many men and women have penned great and noble words, worthy of our consideration. But they are not the words of God unless they are in the Bible. We can never approach other writings like we approach the Bible. It is different in origin, character, and content. All of the Bible was inspired by God and given to complete us and equip us to do God's will (II Timothy 3:16–17). The Bible was written by men who were moved along by the Holy Spirit. They wrote exactly what God wanted them to write (II Peter 1:20–21).

No passage of Scripture better expresses the divine character of the Word of God than Psalm 19:7–11:

> The law of the Lord is perfect, converting the soul;
> The testimony of the Lord is sure, making wise the simple;
> The statutes of the Lord are right, rejoicing the heart;
> The commandment of the Lord is pure, enlightening the eyes;
> The fear of the Lord is clean, enduring forever;
> The judgments of the Lord are true and righteous altogether.
> More to be desired are they than gold, yea, than much fine gold; sweeter also than honey and the honeycomb.
> Moreover by them Your servant is warned, and in keeping them there is great reward.

The further we go into Paul's statement in verse 13, the further we discover what set the Thessalonian church apart from many churches today. We hear the Word. We accept the Word. We walk in the Word. But when it comes to appreciating the Word as from Almighty God, inspired by Him for our benefit, we have fallen behind. The Thessalonians saw the apostles as divine messengers bringing the very words of God to them. We have Paul's words but do not appreciate them the same way. But the Bibles we hold in our hands are as much the Word of God as if God Himself were standing in the pulpit of our church and delivering His words to us. That's what sets the Thessalonians apart from us.

APPLYING THE WORD OF GOD

The living nature of the Word of God is nowhere illustrated better than Paul's last phrase in verse 13: ". . . the word of God, which also effectively works in you who believe." "Effectively works" is from the Greek word *energeo,* which means "to work." But more interestingly, it is the word from which our English word "energy" comes. The Word of God energizes the believer to do the works of God. The New Testament writers almost always used this word to refer to some type of supernatural activity.

Hebrews 4:12 tells us the Word of God is "living and powerful"—it would have to be to "effectively [work] in you who believe." Here are some ways the living Word works in us who believe:

The Word of God Converts Your Soul

Psalm 19:7 says, "The law of the Lord is perfect, converting the soul." It is the Word of God which causes the conversion of the soul, taking a person from a state of non-belief to belief in Jesus Christ. You cannot be saved without the Spirit of God and the Word of God. Both are mandatory. It is the Spirit of God who illumines the heart and allows it to recognize the truth of the Word of God. Whether the truth of the Word of God is read from the Bible, preached from the pulpit, sung in a hymn, read from a tract, or told to someone personally . . . it doesn't matter. Somehow you received the truth from the Word of God into your heart and believed and were saved. To try to convert someone to Christ without conveying to them the Word of God is vain. It is the Word of God which converts the soul.

I have never considered myself an evangelist, or even an evangelistic preacher. But week after week we hear testimonies from our baptistery of people who got saved by hearing the Word of God taught and preached in our church. If we will be faithful to sing, teach, preach, declare, and share the Word of God, souls will be converted.

The Word of God Cleanses Your Life

Note Psalm 119:9: "How can a young man cleanse his way? By taking heed according to Your word." John 15:3 says, "You are already clean because of the word which I have spoken to you." And John 17:17 says, "Sanctify them by Your truth. Your word is truth." The word "sanctify" means to cleanse or to make holy.

When we read the Word of God, that which is different in our lives from what the Word of God says is brought into stark relief. In other words, the sin, immaturity, and foolishness of our lives is revealed—confronted by the Word of God. It is convicting! We want to close the Bible sometimes when we're reading it because we don't like to be shown we're wrong. If you're a Christian, committed to God's best, that experience of being convicted by the Word will cause you to change—to clean up your life, will it not? Remove God's Word from the equation and the cleansing process stops. Reading the Word of God is like a kidney patient being hooked up to a dialysis machine. The blood is cleansed of impurities every time it goes through the dialysis process. So is the heart of the believer cleansed when it connects with the Word of God.

The Word of God Will Control Your Walk

Notice Psalm 119:11: "Your word I have hidden in my heart, That I might not sin against You!" And Psalm 37:31 says, "The law of his God is in his heart; None of his steps shall slide." In the flyleaf of D.L. Moody's Bible were discovered the words, "This book will keep me from sin, or sin will keep me from this book." I don't know if those words originated with D.L. Moody or not, but they are 100 percent accurate. If we allow the Bible into our lives, then our lives will be kept from sin. I don't mean sinless perfection, but as a way of life we will not be practicing sin. But if we sin by ignoring the Word of God, our walk will go in the direction of further sin. Either way, the Bible plays a critical role in the direction of our Christian walk—either toward holiness or away from it.

The Word of God Causes You to Grow

It is impossible to grow as a Christian without a steady diet of the Word of God. When the Apostle Paul was departing Ephesus, saying goodbye to the elders of the church, he said, "So now, brethren, I commend you to God and to the word of His grace which is able to build you up and give you an inheritance among all those who are sanctified" (Acts 20:32). The Apostle Peter said something similar: "As newborn babes, desire the pure milk of the word, that you may grow thereby" (I Peter 2:2). These are basic truths which many Christians learn in the early years of walking with Jesus—but which always bear repeating. It is easy to forget that the Word of God is a *cause* of Christian growth.

The Word of God Counsels Your Decisions

Psalm 19:7–8 says: "The law of the Lord is perfect, converting the soul; the testimony of the Lord is sure, making wise the simple; the statutes of the Lord are right, rejoicing the heart; the commandment of the Lord is pure, enlightening the eyes."

Psalm 73:24 says, "You will guide me with Your counsel, and afterward receive me to glory," and Psalm 119:105 says, "Your word is a lamp to my feet and a light to my path."

When I read the Word of God I am given wisdom from God. If I don't read the Word of God, I do not get God's counsel. God counsels me through His Word. Just as the living Word, Jesus Christ, is named "Wonderful, Counselor" (Isaiah 9:6), so the written Word of God is a counselor as well. The plainest, clearest direction from God comes through His Word.

The Word of God Confirms Your Salvation

Finally, it is the Word of God which establishes in our hearts the conviction that we are saved, that we are forgiven, and that we have an eternal home in heaven. Citing Acts 20:32 again confirms that truth: "Brethren, I commend you to God and to the word of His grace, which is able to build you up and give you an inheritance among all those who are sanctified." One of the ways we are built up (made stronger) is by confidence in our place in God's plan of salvation. We are part of a body of believers God is redeeming for Himself. While confidence is a subjective reality, every true believer testifies that it grows over time as the Word of God is internalized; as hearts and minds are renewed in its truths.

So when we summarize why the Thessalonian church was so dynamic, it is not difficult to suggest it was because of the way they willingly and eagerly embraced the Word of God as brought and taught by the apostles. I get the feeling that they met each new day with a hungry anticipation for what they would hear, learn, or be advised to do from the Word. And, if they had a copy of the Old Testament scrolls, they were probably searching them daily to establish for themselves an understanding of Christ and His fulfillment of Old Covenant prophecies. The Word of God became their life and their lifeline. Through afflictions and suffering of all sorts they became a powerful witness for Christ in their region because of the confidence they had in the truth of the Word. Who would not be empowered to stand strong if everything the Bible teaches were taken to heart and believed just as it is written?

We could use Paul's words to Titus as a guide: Have we "adorn[ed] the doctrine of God our Savior in all things?" (Titus 2:10) We adorn the Word of God by the way we allow it to change our lives from the inside out. As our lives become conformed to the written Word, we become more like the living Word. Have you spent time in the Word today? May I encourage you to do so, that the doctrine of God may be adorned ever more beautifully through your life.

APPLICATION

1. Read Deuteronomy 6:4–9; 11:18–21.

    a. Most intimately, where were the Israelites supposed to carry God's words and laws? (verses 6:6; 11:18a)

    b. How were their children to learn God's words? (verses 6:7; 11:19)

    c. What small difference in wording is found regarding teaching in verses 6:7 and 11:19?

    d. What is the difference between "teach" and "teach diligently" (NKJV), or "impress" and "teach (NIV)?

    e. If a stranger spent a week in your home, what evidence would he find that you are teaching God's Word to your children diligently?

f. What might be the difference in the average Christian home between "teaching" and "impressing" God's Word upon the heart of children?

g. How do you interpret the meaning of the further instructions about teaching children? (verses 6:7; 11:19) Are these literal ways to teach or are these illustrative words? If the latter, what do they mean?

h. What is the meaning of the rest of the instructions? (verses 6:8–9; 11:18b, 20–21)

i. From both of these passages, describe in your own words the role to be played by the Word of God in the average Israelite family:

j. What was the purpose of all these instructions? (verse 11:21)

k. How would you translate this Old Testament blessing into something similar for the New Testament Christian? That is, what is the purpose of embracing the Word of God today?

2. Psalm 119 is a psalm extolling the virtues and benefits of the Word of God. From the following 10 verses note the benefit which accrues from embracing God's precepts as contained in His Word:

   a. Psalm 119:9

   b. Psalm 119:11

   c. Psalm 119:24

   d. Psalm 119:45

   e. Psalm 119:92

f. Psalm 119:99

g. Psalm 119:127–128

h. Psalm 119:130

i. Psalm 119:165

j. Psalm 119:171–172

3. Who was Ezra? (Ezra 7:10)

   a. What had the Israelites lacked while they were in captivity in Babylon? (Nehemiah 8:1)

b. What did Ezra do to remedy their deficiency? (Nehemiah 8:2–3)

c. How long did he read, and did the people listen? (Nehemiah 8:3)

d. How did the people listen? (Nehemiah 8:3b)

e. What impact does the presence of our many Bibles have on our hunger for the Word? How would it be different if they were taken away?

DID YOU KNOW?

The Greek word Paul used in Titus 2:10 for "adorn" is the verb *kosmeo*. It, along with other words in the same family ("orderly," "world ruler," "pertaining to the world") all derive from the word *kosmos*. Everyone recognizes "cosmos," even it its Greek form. The cosmos is the ordered world system in which we live. While it can refer to a negative or positive world system, its primary meaning is "order." When we "order" our lives according to God's will as revealed in Scripture, we reflect, or attribute order to, the doctrine of God. Our lives are to have the same stability and order that is characteristic of a world system— and they will when they are ordered according to God's Word.

LESSON 5

THE BROTHERHOOD OF SUFFERING

I Thessalonians 2:14–20

In this lesson we discover the powerful bonds between fellow believers.

OUTLINE

When people think of their best friends, it is usually in the context of shared joy—recreational experiences, mutual interests, years-long relationships. But Paul reveals bonds that are built quickly, go deeper, and last for eternity—in spite of Satan's best efforts to stop them.

I. **Encouraging His Suffering Brothers**
   A. They Prosecuted the Lord Jesus and the Prophets
   B. They Persecuted the Christians
   C. They Pleased Not God
   D. They Pursued All Men
   E. They Prohibited God's Message from Being Shared
   F. They Pushed God's Patience to the Ultimate

II. **Explaining His Separation from His Brothers**
   A. Satan Can Delay the Answers to Your Prayers
   B. Satan Can Deceive You Through False Teachers
   C. Satan Can Defeat You in Your Attempts to Walk with God
   D. Satan Can Discourage You by Afflicting Your Body
   E. Satan Can Devour You and Your Influence for God

III. **Expressing His Satisfaction with the Believers**

OVERVIEW

If you have read anything at all of church history—even the brief biblical account in the book of Acts—you know that faith always prospers during times of persecution. Then, it often disappears when everything is going well. George Everett Ross has observed there are basically two kinds of faith: The "if" kind and the "though" kind. The first says "If everything goes well . . . I will believe in God." The latter says, "Though evil prospers . . . I will cling to God for my salvation." It was Job who had the second kind of faith: "Though He slay me, yet will I trust Him" (Job 13:15a).

Ross's observation prompts us to examine our own faith, especially at the beginning of this particular lesson. Is my faith the "if" kind or the "though" kind? If you are a Christian, eventually your life will be tested to an extent that, if you have only an "if" kind of faith, your faith will be decimated. You will feel as though all is lost. Eventually, every Christian who perseveres to the end must develop a "though" kind of faith. You must learn to trust the Lord even in times of suffering and despair.

The Christians at Thessalonica had the second kind of faith—the "though" kind. They had stood the test of persecution and suffering for their faith, yet continued to declare the Gospel. We have seen already that they took the Gospel to the neighboring regions of Macedonia. But what we tend to overlook is that their outreach came in the face of intense persecution. When they were placed under great pressure, they responded with faithfulness. They allowed adversity to be a motivating factor in their lives.

In the last verses of chapter two of First Thessalonians we find Paul commending the faith of the Thessalonian church. He first encourages his suffering brothers, then explains his separation from them, then expresses his satisfaction with them.

ENCOURAGING HIS SUFFERING BROTHERS (2:14-16)

The church in Jerusalem was thought of by all the other churches as the one that had suffered the most. Persecution arose there first; indeed, Paul himself had been part of the Jewish persecution of the infant church in Jerusalem. But he tells the Thessalonians that they, by their willingness to suffer at the hands of their countrymen, have gained equal honor with the Jerusalem church.

The Thessalonian church, located in Macedonia, was made up primarily of Gentiles. Though this was not the time of the great persecutions which would later come under Emperor Nero, by whose hand Paul himself died, there was still great antagonism among the Gentiles—and even the Jews in Macedonia—toward the Christian church. The believers in Thessalonica were suffering at the hands of their countrymen just as the Jewish believers had suffered at the hands of their countrymen in Israel. Across the Mediterranean, there was a kinship between the Jewish church in Jerusalem and the Gentile church in Thessalonica. Suffering draws believers together.

If the body of Christ in America were going through some sort of persecution, or if another kind of suffering were widespread, the churches in America would be full. I recall when the Persian Gulf War fighting began in January, 1991, attendance at the church I pastor went up around 20 percent for about two months. Then as the fighting stopped and tensions began to ease, attendance went back to its normal levels. It is interesting how tribulation and suffering, even when it is half a world away, brings people together and makes us aware of our need for God. This was seen in America most noticeably, of course, in the wake of the September 11, 2001, terrorist attacks in New York City and Washington, D.C. America's willingness to become openly religious in a time of great need reminded one of the days of the founding fathers.

A willingness to suffer is one of the proofs of true Christian discipleship. There is no such thing as being a Christian and not having some kind of suffering—either the kind of sufferings that all humans experience or suffering directly related to your faith. This is not morbidity, it is realism. Anyone who becomes a Christian thinking they will be spared suffering by God is in for a rude awakening. The Apostle Paul wrote to his young protégé in the faith, Timothy, to warn him of this very truth: "Yes, and all who desire to live godly in Christ Jesus will suffer persecution" (II Timothy 3:12). No might, not maybe—but will. Jesus Christ taught His disciples the same thing in John 15:20 and 16:33.

One of the greatest paradoxes in church history is that the Apostle Paul had been such a vehement persecutor of the church as a Pharisee (Acts 9:1–2, 13; Galatians 1:13). He knew all too well the bitter hatred that the Jews had for the Christian church since he was one of the leaders of the Jewish attacks. Early leaders in the church were direct targets of persecution of the church. Stephen, James, and Peter came under attack directly or through the efforts of political rulers like Herod (Acts 12:3).

So Paul knew what the believers in Thessalonica were experiencing. We mentioned in earlier lessons the record in Acts 17 of the Jewish attacks on the apostles and those who had become believers (Acts 17:5 ff.). The Jews turned their vengeance on those who were hosting the apostles in the city, claiming that all were defying Caesar's decree that only he should be worshipped as divine king. Of course, the apostles made no references to Caesar in their preaching; these were the allegations of desperate opponents of the Gospel.

In verse 15 Paul does a unique thing—he catalogs the sins of the Jews against Christ and His messengers:

They Prosecuted the Lord Jesus and the Prophets

Paul says it was the Jews who killed the Lord Jesus Christ and the prophets of Israel. They are not any more guilty than the Romans or us, for that matter. But they were the ones, historically, who instigated the false charges against Christ. John 1:11 says, "He came to His own, and His own did not receive Him." The death of Christ was the culmination of a long line of attacks upon the prophets sent by God. Because the Jews didn't like the message God was sending, they attacked the messengers, thinking the message would go away. Indeed, the message only became louder with each prophet who was killed until the message came in person—Jesus Christ, the living Word of God.

I read of a missionary who took the Gospel message to a primitive tribe of natives who did not know the Gospel. He prepared a chart as a visual aid that showed the progress of a man who accepted Christ as he made his way to heaven and the progress of the man who rejected Christ as he went to hell. The tribe was so upset by this message that they jumped up and destroyed the chart! They thought by burning the chart they could negate what they had just been taught. But the truth doesn't go away just because you destroy the delivery mechanism or the messenger. But that is what the Jews did to Christ. They didn't like being told they were hypocrites and seeing many of those who were their "subjects" becoming followers of an uneducated carpenter from Nazareth. So they tried to destroy Him.

They Persecuted the Christians

Notice the phrase: "and have persecuted us." The "Judeans," the Jews in Jerusalem, killed Jesus and the prophets before Him, and also persecuted any who tried to believe in Him, which included Paul and the apostles after he became a believer himself.

They Pleased Not God

It is amazing that religious people can be absolutely convinced they are doing the will of God when they are doing the exact opposite. Paul says in verse 15 that the Jews did not please God in what they did—even though they thought they were doing God's will. The Jews are not the only ones in history guilty of not pleasing God. In the name of Christ, movements such as the Crusades and the Inquisitions in Europe employed murderous tactics at times to do things not pleasing to God. It is the height of deception to claim to be acting in God's name when God is in no way pleased with the acts. People who commit such acts are more focused on pleasing themselves than on pleasing God.

They Pursued All Men

Paul next says the Jews were "contrary to all men." Interestingly, the Jews in the ancient world were accused of hating the human race. Because they were the chosen people of God, they allowed arrogance to take the place of humility. They thought themselves to be chosen for privilege instead of for service. They felt the world was destined to serve them instead of them serving the world. So they found themselves at odds with everyone who was not a Jew—and with God.

They Prohibited God's Message from Being Shared

The Jews didn't want the Gentiles to be told they could be saved, that they were inheritors of the covenant promises given to Abraham. Therefore, Paul says, they tried to keep the apostles from speaking to the Gentiles "that they may be saved" (verse 16). Whether in Jerusalem or in Macedonia, the Jews tried to hinder the progress of the Gospel to the Gentiles. Rather than being willing to share the bountiful grace of God with the world, the Jews tried to hoard it and keep the blessings for themselves.

They Pushed God's Patience to the Ultimate

The conclusion of Paul's list of sins which Israel committed is to declare that they had filled up "the measure of their sins; but wrath has come upon them to the uttermost" (verse 16). This means their actions had become a matter of record and God had responded by allowing all men to see the evidence of Israel's sins.

They were a matter of record both with Him and with the nations. Therefore, when God responded in judgment there would be no doubt as to Israel's guilt. It is as if a cauldron were being filled with Israel's sins, filled to overflowing. No one would say her judgment was undeserved.

God, while overflowing with grace, does have a limit to His patience. Though we sometimes look out at the world and wonder how long sin will be allowed to continue (seemingly) unchecked, we must remember that God is keeping His books. His longsuffering and patience allows men to go without punishment, always wanting them to come to repentance. But the day of judgment will come according to His timetable.

It is amazing to see Paul speaking with such clarity concerning the sins of his own people. That he would denounce the Jews so forcefully leaves no doubt as to the extent they had departed from God's ways. The declaration of the wrath of God upon them was a foreboding statement of judgment upon a people who had resisted the grace of God—and were now trying to prevent others from receiving it as well.

Paul now turns to the Thessalonians and explains the reason for his having to depart from them and his delay in returning to them. His words give insight into the spiritual dynamics undergirding what we might call "scheduling conflicts."

Explaining His Separation from His Brothers (2:17–18)

For a reason unknown to us, Paul was forced to leave Thessalonica, prompting the letters to them which we are studying in these lessons. His words indicate that his and his fellow workers' leaving was not voluntary—they were "taken away" (verse 17). This phrase literally means to be "orphaned." Paul first compared himself to a mother, then to a father, and now to an orphan in that he was involuntarily separated from those he loved in Thessalonica. "We were orphaned from you," he is saying.

The more complex issue concerning his absence from Thessalonica comes in verse 18. Paul declares he had wanted to return to Thessalonica more than once—but Satan hindered him. Many believers have questions about how far Satan can go in influencing the life of a believer in Christ. Does he have access to my life? What power does he have over me? If Satan can hinder the activities of the great Apostle Paul, what must he be able to do to one such as me?

The word "hinder" is a military term, used to describe the disruption of roads and bridges which would slow the progress of an invading army. In a similar way, Satan had done something to slow the movement of the Apostle Paul. Paul wanted to return to Thessalonica but had been unable to do so. In order that we better understand our relationship to our Enemy, I have listed a number of ways that Satan can hinder the work of a believer.

Satan Can Delay the Answers to Your Prayers

We have biblical evidence to support the fact that Satan can indeed work behind the scenes in the realm of spiritual warfare to delay the answers to our prayers. In the book of Daniel we find that great man of God praying and going three weeks without an answer. But we also have this revelation: "But the prince of the kingdom of Persia withstood me twenty-one days; and behold, Michael, one of the chief princes, came to help me for I had been left alone there with the kings of Persia" (Daniel 10:13). These are the words of an angelic messenger who had been sent with the answer to Daniel's prayer on the very day he began to pray. But apparently a demonic angel, the prince of the kingdom of Persia, had interfered with the messenger's mission. Without the help of the chief angel, Michael, the messenger might not have gotten through at all.

Sometimes when we pray we may wonder why there has been no answer. Something may be going on behind the scenes of which you are unaware. There could be a spiritual conflict hindering the answer to your prayer.

Satan Can Deceive You Through False Teachers

Second Corinthians 11:13–15 says, "For such are false apostles, deceitful workers, transforming themselves into apostles of Christ. And no wonder! For Satan himself transforms himself into an angel of light. Therefore it is no great thing if his ministers also transform themselves into ministers of righteousness, whose end will be according to their works." Not every minister is a minister of God. Paul clearly says that some ministers are agents of Satan who disguise themselves to appear as ministers of righteousness.

Satan Can Defeat You in Your Attempts to Walk with God

In Acts 5, we have the story of Ananias and Sapphira attempting to lie in the presence of the Holy Spirit, an act motivated by Satan: "Ananias, why has Satan filled your heart to lie to the Holy Spirit . . ." (Acts 5:3). They lied to the apostles, men operating under the guidance of the Holy Spirit, about how much money they received from the sale of their property. And it was Satan who laid that possibility before them (see also II Corinthians 2:11; 11:3; I Timothy 5:15).

Satan Can Discourage You by Afflicting Your Body

I mention this one with some hesitancy because I don't want to suggest that any time someone is sick it's the result of Satan's work. That is undoubtedly not true. But he does have the power to afflict our bodies. In the experience of Job, his physical maladies were as a direct result of the actions of Satan against his body (Job 2:7). It's also important to note that Satan's actions were carried out with God's permission. Satan is not a free agent; he is under God's ultimate control. Satan was a tool in God's hand to accomplish a deeper purpose in Job's life.

Satan Can Devour You and Your Influence for God

Peter warned believers in the first century to "Be sober; be vigilant; because your adversary the devil walks about like a roaring lion, seeking whom he may devour" (I Peter 5:8). In the Greek language, "devour" meant to take away a person's influence by consuming that person. If Satan can remove our influence, he doesn't have to remove us. We could be distracted, discouraged, or defeated in other ways and thereby be "devoured" insofar as our influence goes.

Did Satan use any of these tactics to hinder the Apostle Paul from returning to Thessalonica? He certainly could have, but we do not know for sure. We only know that Satan hindered him. And therein lies the message for the believer today: Satan is in the business of hindering the saints of God, one way or the other. We need to be sober, vigilant, on the alert, in prayer, and clothed with the armor of God, standing against the wiles of the devil. The surest way to be hindered by Satan is to think he does not have the power to do so. If we resist his efforts, he will flee from us (James 4:7).

One of the most effective ways for us to hinder Satan is to praise the Lord. Satan does not like praise and worship. If our praise is genuine, we are acknowledging the Lordship of Christ in our lives. The more focused we are on the Lordship of Christ, the less likely we are to be distracted or deceived by Satan's temptations.

Though Paul has not been able to get back to Thessalonica at the time of his writing this letter, he is still overjoyed at the reports of their progress. We close this lesson with a look at verses 19–20 and the expression of Paul's joy.

EXPRESSING HIS SATISFACTION WITH THE BELIEVERS (2:19-20)

If you had the chance to choose a crown for yourself, what would it be? For Paul, it was knowing that those he had led to Christ were living a life of commitment to Christ: "You are our hope, you are our joy, you are our crown of rejoicing." Knowing that the Thessalonians would one day appear in the presence of the Lord Jesus Christ at His coming would be the zenith of Paul's existence as a Christian and an apostle. Nothing brought him greater joy than such anticipation.

Robert Moffat, the 19th century Scottish missionary to Africa, when asked to sign a young woman's album (like a memoir or autograph book), he wrote the following:

My album is a savage breast
Where tempests brood and shadows rest
Without one ray of light.
To write the name of Jesus there
And see that savage bow in prayer
And point to worlds more bright and fair,
This is my soul's delight.

The greatest delight for Robert Moffat was to see an untamed human heart transformed into the heart of a man who knows Jesus and who bows before Him. That's exactly the sentiment of the Apostle Paul. He went into Thessalonica, a pagan city filled with idol worship and savage sentiments, and preached the Gospel of the grace of God. Those who believed became brand new people with lives changed by God. That's exactly what Paul is saying to the Thessalonian believers. He doesn't anticipate a crown for his work with them—*they* are his crown!

We are going to discover as we get further into these two epistles that the second coming of Christ is a primary topic for Paul with this church. I am continually amazed at how something which was a constant subject with Paul is rarely mentioned in many so-called Bible teaching churches. Paul was very much concerned that Christians whom he ministered to live their lives in light of the return of Christ. In a sense, life on this earth was viewed by Paul as lived in anticipation of the eternal life which would begin following Christ's return. And Paul viewed the Thessalonians as a crown which would be made manifest at that time.

The question for us is, Who is there that will be a crown in our lives on the day of Christ's return? Who will be there glorying in the return of Christ because we invested time and resources in their life spiritually? Will heaven be populated with people we have led to Christ or discipled or ministered to in some way? For Paul, he viewed those in the churches he planted that way—people who were like a crown to him, the crowning achievement of his life.

Satan may have hindered Paul's attempts to return to Thessalonica, but there was no way Satan could hinder his reunion with the Thessalonians at the return of Christ. Just as there was joy when each of the Thessalonians individually accepted Christ (Luke 15:10) so Paul anticipated a day of great joy when he would be reunited with them before the throne of Christ to live together for eternity.

As we close this lesson, think about those who invested time in your life to make sure your baby steps became mature steps spiritually. You will be a crown for those people one day. Then think of those who may become your crown. Your children, a neighbor, those in a Sunday school class, and maybe, like Paul, those on a mission field you have won to Christ. May God give us the hunger for future joy by investing ourselves in the lives of growing Christians today.

APPLICATION

1. Read Matthew 23:33–39.

    a. Compare Jesus' words in verse 33b with I Thessalonians 2:16b. What are Jesus and Paul saying about the "fate" of the Jews?

    b. Who was Jesus going to send to the Jews? (verse 34)

    c. What were the Jews going to do to these people? (verse 34)

    d. Why was Jesus going to send prophets to the Jews if He knew the Jews would persecute and kill them? (verse 35)

    e. How does Paul's statement, "to fill up the measure of their sins" (I Thessalonians 2:16) help you understand what Jesus is doing?

    f. For the death of how many prophets is God holding the Jews responsible? (verse 35)

    g. How was that judgment brought upon the generation of Jews to whom Jesus was speaking? (verse 36)

h. Why was God justified in ultimately bringing judgment upon the Jews? (verse 37)

i. The Roman general Titus destroyed Jerusalem and the Temple in 70 A.D. How did that destruction fulfill Jesus' final prophecy about the Jews? (verses 38–39)

2. From the following verses, describe Paul's activity as one who opposed the spread of the Gospel:

   a. Acts 8:3

   b. Acts 9:13

   c. Acts 9:14

   d. Acts 9:21

   e. Acts 22:4

   f. Acts 22:5

g. Galatians 1:13, 23

h. Describe any efforts at opposing the Gospel of true Christianity on your part before becoming a Christian:

i. What insight do your own experiences give you now in reaching others for Christ?

3. Read 2 Corinthians 2:5–11.

   a. What is the topic of these verses? (verses 8, 10)

   b. What warning does Paul give the Corinthians in verse 11?

   c. What could Satan do in this situation to "hinder" the work of the church?

   d. How does this make you think differently about times when you are tempted not to forgive or extend love to someone who has sinned?

4. What does II Corinthians 10:3–5 tell you about the nature of combating Satan's schemes?

a. In what realm do Satan's hindrances often arise? (verse 5a)

b. How do you overcome those hindrances? (verse 5b)

c. Describe any work for God in which you are being hindered now (or in the recent past):

d. Can you assign the hindrance to Satan? Why or why not?

e. What is the best way for you to remove it and accomplish the work?

DID YOU KNOW?

The crown which Paul anticipated wearing is not a regal crown fit for a king or ruler. That is the word *diadema*, from which we get our word diadem, or crown. Instead, the crown Paul refers to in I Thessalonians 2:19 is a *stephanos*, from *stepho*, to encircle. This crown, or more often translated "wreath," was the one awarded to Greek athletes for winning an athletic contest. And Paul clearly makes use of it in that sense as well (I Corinthians 9:25), comparing the Christian life to a race. That is the sense he implies here. If the Thessalonians complete the course, remaining faithful to Christ until His return, they will be like a victor's garland for Paul on that day. Unlike the wreaths won by athletes, however, the Thessalonians would be a wreath which would never fade away.

LESSON 6

GROWING UP IN YOUR FAITH

I Thessalonians 3:1–13

In this lesson we learn the central role of faith in building the church.

OUTLINE

How many different programs do churches engage in to build their numbers and strengthen their standing as a body? All of them probably have merit—if they have one ingredient at their core. Besides bringing us to God, faith is the reality that keeps us in Him despite all obstacles.

I. **Faith and Persistent Trials**
   A. Trials Are to Be Expected
   B. Trials Are to Be an Evaluation
   C. Trials Are to Be Endured

II. **Faith and Personal Temptation**

III. **Faith and Practical Thoughtfulness**
   A. Their Faith Bound Them Together in Fellowship
   B. Their Fellowship Built Them Up in the Faith

IV. **Faith and Patient Toil**

V. **Faith and Prayerful Transformation**
   A. How to Pray for New Believers
   B. What to Pray for New Believers

OVERVIEW

The first church I pastored consisted of my wife, myself, and a few families. We figured the church wouldn't grow by attracting Christians since we were so small. So we decided to reach out to non-Christians instead. We trained ourselves in the use of the Evangelism Explosion materials and began to see people come to Christ. Some Thursday nights our group would see eight, ten, or twelve people come to Christ in one evening. It was a marvelous time of watching God honor the Gospel, and the church began to grow.

But one day a man in our church, a godly man whom I greatly respected, took me to lunch and said, "David, you're teaching the church to be obstetricians but we don't have any pediatricians. We're bringing lots of new baby Christians into the world but we don't have anyone to take care of them and train them in Christian living." He was exactly right, so we began using a follow-up program designed to disciple new believers—and guess what happened: Since we were so small, we didn't have enough mature believers to have two teams—an evangelism team and a discipleship team. So everybody that had been doing evangelism started doing discipleship and we stopped winning people to Christ.

I learned through that experience what a delicate balance exists between bringing people into the faith and then building them up in the faith. In I Thessalonians, chapter one, we read about the Thessalonians getting saved. Then in chapter two we read about them beginning to serve. But in chapter three, beginning with this lesson, we're going to see Paul's concern for their sanctification—growing up in the Lord and developing a holy life. It is a classic passage of Scripture on how to help those young in the faith grow into spiritual maturity.

The setting is this: Paul had, for some reason unknown to us, been removed from Thessalonica (he is writing this letter from Corinth). We saw in the last lesson how he had been hindered by Satan from returning to Thessalonica to continue his ministry there. He wanted to check on their spiritual progress, to make sure they were still strong in the Lord. In lieu of his own ability to get to Thessalonica, he sent Timothy to them. Timothy has returned to Paul and brought a welcome report that the believers in Thessalonica are continuing in faith and love (3:6).

Faith, in fact, is the key to chapter three—it occurs five times (verses 2, 5, 6, 7, 10). In this lesson, we will focus on the relationship of faith to five realities in the spiritual life: trials, temptation, thoughtfulness, toil, and transformation.

FAITH AND PERSISTENT TRIALS (3:2-4)

The reason Paul sent Timothy to Thessalonica was to encourage the believers concerning their faith (3:2). Paul was worried that the trials they were experiencing would rock them off the foundation of their faith (3:3). The faith of new believers needs to be established (strengthened) and encouraged. Nothing can be more discouraging to a new believer than to be thrown into the midst of trials. It seems the Enemy always takes the opportunity to afflict new believers with trouble or tribulation to try to wrest their faith from them in the beginning. If there is not someone there to strengthen and encourage a new believer, doubts about their faith can set in. They can even give up on the faith.

Paul knew that Timothy, though he was a young man, was an outsider to the Thessalonians—and sometimes that's what it takes. An objective person who can come in from the outside and be a source of strength can often save the day. Timothy didn't go to teach theology or give a lecture. He went to be an encourager, to build up the saints in what they had received from Paul. It was important for the believers to hear that the truth they had received from Paul was in fact the truth; that tribulation didn't mean it wasn't the truth; and that by standing in that truth they would survive the tests they were undergoing. A knowledge of biblical truth is the most important ingredient in withstanding tribulation and tests. Timothy was a trusted protégé of Paul and had been sent by him to other churches on similar missions as that to the Thessalonians (I Corinthians 16:10-11; Philippians 2:19).

Believers who are not strengthened in the midst of tests can be "shaken by [their] afflictions" (3:3). The word "shaken" is used outside the New Testament to describe a dog wagging its tail; a word which at its root means to fawn over, or to flatter. Paul was afraid that somehow the Thessalonians were going to yield to being fawned over or flattered by opponents of the faith; perhaps talked out of their faith in the absence of the apostles. No doubt the Jews who opposed the faith in Thessalonica (Acts 17:5) were trying to convince the believers that if they would give up the faith, their troubles would go away.

We need a theology of adversity in the church today. Most of what we have is a theology of prosperity which tells believers that God wants them to have all they need *and* all they want. But that is false doctrine and will not sustain the Christian in times of trouble. Three truths concerning adversity need to undergird every believer's faith.

Trials Are to Be Expected

A well-known book about the spiritual dimensions of life begins with these words: "Life is difficult." Very few mature people would disagree with that statement. But somehow the typical new Christian thinks that life is not supposed to be difficult once they accept Jesus as their Savior. Nothing could be more unbiblical. In fact, it was the Apostle Peter who said, "Beloved, do not think it strange concerning the fiery trial which is to try you, as though some strange thing happened to you" (I Peter 4:12). It's not strange; it's normal. In a community panel discussion I participated in on suffering with diseases, I was asked the question, "Why did you get cancer?" My answer was, "Because I'm human." Illness and disease are part of the human condition. Being a Christian doesn't exempt one from being human.

Trials Are to Be an Evaluation

First Peter 1:6–7 says, "In this you greatly rejoice, though now for a little while, if need be, you have been grieved by various trials, that the genuineness of your faith, being much more precious than gold that perishes, though it is tested by fire, may be found to praise, honor, and glory at the revelation of Jesus Christ." Trials are treasures from God which can either make us bitter or better. If we accept trials for what they are—experiences which can strengthen us—they can refine our faith and transform us in the process. Trials are transient. But in the time they are with us, if we will let them have their purpose, they can be like mini-schools in which we are graduated to a higher level of maturity.

Trials Are to Be Endured

I had an encounter recently with two different people on the matter of enduring trials. One person was involved in a ministry that goes into countries where Christians are being persecuted and rescues them from that persecution. The next day I spoke with another believer who is involved in a ministry that believes what the first ministry is doing is wrong—that we have no right to go into countries where Christians are being persecuted and remove them. Their argument is that it removes the presence of Christ from that country and—and this is the point relative to our discussion in this lesson—*where does it say we should try to escape trials when we can?*

The Bible certainly gives indication that enduring, rather than escaping, trials should be the believer's goal (Hebrews 12:7; James 1:3–7). I am the first to admit that there may be redemptive value in removing an individual(s) from a certain trial. But the point Scripture makes is that trials are common to us all and we should learn to live life in the midst of trials rather than thinking trials are an exception to life and we don't deserve to have to go through them. One aspect of the fruit of the Spirit is patience, and there simply is no way to develop patience apart from trials in our lives (which is a good reason to be careful when you pray for patience!).

FAITH AND PERSONAL TEMPTATION (3:5)

Verse 5 clearly states Paul's reason for sending Timothy to Thessalonica—he was afraid Satan would get his hooks into the Thessalonian believers and draw them away from the faith. If that happened, Paul's work in that city would ultimately have been in vain.

A believer's greatest vulnerability to spiritual attack is the time following his conversion before getting grounded in spiritual truth—especially the truth that trials are a normal part of human existence which do not go away when you become a Christian. Religious cults thrive on recruiting new Christian believers—and there were religious cults in Paul's day just as there are in ours. New Christians are enthusiastic and energetic and eager to please, but often don't know enough to guard against becoming entrapped in false doctrine. Therefore, they are prime targets for those seeking to pull the unaware into a web of religious error. One of the strongest passages on this in the New Testament is Galatians 1:6–9 where Paul expressed strong concern over the believers in Galatia wandering away from the truth of their newfound faith. The believers there were new in the faith and were already being tempted by a syncretistic blend of Judaism and Christianity. They were like lambs being surrounded by ravenous wolves.

Part of the responsibility of older Christians who bring new converts into the faith is to guard them until they can stand on their own. To be aggressive in evangelism without being aggressive in follow-up is to run the risk of bringing new believers in the front door only to have them wander untended out the back door (as my friend years ago warned me). This is the immediate context of Peter's famous warning to the believers in Asia Minor: Satan is afoot, going about "like a roaring lion, seeking whom he may devour" (I Peter 5:8).

I recall an illustration used by Dr. James Dobson when the Focus on the Family ministry was reeling from some difficult experiences regarding inappropriate, and in one case immoral, actions by some of their staff. The inappropriate behavior by two highly visible leaders in their ministry had attracted nationwide attention and brought the entire ministry under criticism and scrutiny—both within the church and without. In a message to the organization's staff, Dr. Dobson raised the issue of why there is so much sin and disruption in the world, even within churches and ministries, if Satan was judged at the cross. Why do we still see the effects of his temptations if he is a defeated foe? To illustrate his answer he told a story of a missionary who had been away from his hut in the jungles of Africa for a few days. When he returned to his home he was shocked to discover a huge jungle snake on the floor of his simple hut. The snake was much too large to dispatch by hand, so he returned to his truck and got his pistol which had only one bullet in it. He fired at the head of the snake and mortally wounded it, though the snake did not die instantly. Instead, it flopped and flailed itself around in the inside of the hut and made a wreck of everything before it finally died a few hours later. Dr. Dobson concluded the illustration by saying, "Our enemy Satan has been mortally wounded, and these are his last days, and he is flopping around with all that he has, trying to destroy everything that can bring glory and honor to Jesus Christ who is the One who pronounced his death sentence."

Satan is still alive and destroying peoples' lives today. Even though his death sentence was pronounced at the cross and resurrection of Christ, he is still "flopping around" doing everything he can to wreak havoc on the human race, and especially in the body of Christ. Paul, the same one who warns against the tactics of the devil, says we do not have to fear temptation (I Corinthians 10:13), that God will provide a way of escape. Our job is to stay vigilant and sober regarding the reality of the temptation and be obedient to take the way of escape He provides.

FAITH AND PRACTICAL THOUGHTFULNESS (3:6, 8)

In verses 6 and 8 Paul recaps the mutual exchange of love and faith between himself and the Thessalonians, and cites the relationship between fellowship and faith.

Their Faith Bound Them Together in Fellowship

The pronouns tell the story. Paul uses "us" and "we" a total of five times and "you" and "your" four times to describe the interconnectedness of him and the Thessalonians. There was much fellowship and growth occurring in the church at Thessalonica and in the intermediated relationship between Paul and the believers. It was faith that bound them together and provided the basis for their fellowship.

I can't imagine being all alone as a Christian. Some people have found themselves in those circumstances in their lives, and it is not easy. Fellowship is one of those privileges which we probably take for granted until we don't have it. Then we realize what a vital part of our spiritual life it is. Those Christians who have the opportunity to take advantage of Christian fellowship, but don't, are missing a great blessing and an indispensable part of mature Christian living. I was encouraged recently to learn that our church has 122 small groups consisting of 1,367 people meeting around our area. And we're still tracking down ones we don't know about yet! Fellowship takes on a life of its own as people bind themselves together in groups around a common faith.

Their Fellowship Built Them Up in the Faith

Faith is the basis of fellowship, but fellowship strengthens and builds faith to the next level. When you pile hot coals over and around one another, they provide a greater amount of heat than if they were all burning separately. In fact, take a coal out of the fire and set it by itself and it will soon go out. Getting separated from fellowship is a sure way for faith to grow weak.

FAITH AND PATIENT TOIL (3:7)

"Faith" surfaces again in verse 7. While the focus has been on the afflictions and suffering of the Thessalonian believers, Paul hints at the fact that he is undergoing affliction as well: "In all our affliction and distress we were comforted concerning you by your faith." Whatever Paul was undergoing, the faith of the Thessalonian church was like a shot in the arm to his own faith. It made him want to keep on.

Believers today have lost the ability to toil patiently in the faith. Since we are not required to toil patiently at many other things in life, we have developed the perspective that the spiritual life should be accomplished as quickly as our "instant breakfast" drink we mix in the morning. Whereas our ancestors were content to wait a week for the next stagecoach coming through if they missed this week's, we are not so patient. If we don't switch to another flight that leaves within the hour, we rocket off an email, fax, phone call, or page. It's just the way our life works. But sometimes the spiritual life doesn't work that way, and we are required to toil patiently before seeing changes or results.

It has become common in churches today not to expect a commitment to serve for any longer than one year at a time. People just seem not to be able to envision staying at something longer than that period of time. Yet our commitment to Christ is a lifetime commitment! I have even grown increasingly suspicious of the entire concept of retirement. I can find no biblical support for the idea of ceasing productive work for the last 20 years of life. If we do stop doing our career work after a certain age, we ought to be willing to sign up for new service for the Lord instead of thinking we've earned the right to do nothing. The most underutilized resource in the church is those in the "retirement" years who are not being challenged to bring their wisdom, skills, experience, and time to bear upon challenges and opportunities in ministry.

Standing fast and toiling patiently were characteristic of the Thessalonians, and Paul was greatly encouraged by their commitment.

FAITH AND PRAYERFUL TRANSFORMATION (3:9–13)

The best way Paul knew to thank the Thessalonians for their steadfast faith was to pray for them (verse 10). There are numerous needs which new believers have which can be met effectively through continual prayer.

How to Pray for New Believers

After studying this passage of Scripture, I became convicted that churches should be active in praying for the needs of new believers.

1. We are to pray thankfully. "For what thanks can we render to God for you . . ." (verse 9). Before he even began to pray for the Thessalonian believers Paul gave thanks for them and their faith. We are to pray thanking God for new believers in Christ.
2. We are to pray joyfully. "For all the joy with which we rejoice for your sake before our God" (verse 9). Next, Paul expressed joy before God for the Thessalonians. Thankfulness for their salvation and joy in their steadfast faith.
3. We are to pray continually. "Night and day" (verse 10). All day long Paul had the Thessalonians in his heart. Working on tents, walking in the streets, worshiping with the saints . . . the Thessalonians were the object of his prayerful concern. Paul's life seemed to be a continual conversation with God, and he never ceased lifting up the new believers in Thessalonica. He assumed the responsibility for their spiritual sustenance as much as he did their salvation.
4. We are to pray fervently. "Praying exceedingly" (verse 10). The word "exceedingly" is rare in the New Testament (here; Ephesians 3:20; I Thessalonians 5:13) and means "exceedingly abundantly" or "most earnestly." Paul didn't just pray for the Thessalonians—he prayed earnestly and beyond what we might imagine or think.
5. We are to pray specifically. There are a number of things new believers need more than mature believers. We should make our prayers specific to those ends.

What to Pray for New Believers

1. Pray for the perfection of their faith. "That we may see your face and perfect what is lacking in your faith" (verse 10). First, pray for the perfection of their faith. These new believers didn't know very much; they were not very mature. They needed to be discipled—taught the Bible (the Old Testament), taught how to pray, taught how to defend their faith. Whatever was lacking in their faith would hinder their growth and cause them to be lacking as believers. So their faith needed to be perfected, or made mature. Little faith means little growth, and little growth means little service.

J. I. Packer has noted six characteristics of maturity; not necessarily spiritual maturity, but maturity in general.

1) Ability to face reality. Do we live in denial about reality, or are we mature enough to face reality regardless of what it brings?

2) Ability to adapt to change. Immature people resist change; mature people expect change as a normal part of life.

3) Freedom from tension and anxiety. Mature people have a steady perspective on life; they don't get easily rattled or unnerved. For the Christian this means a confident trust in the plan of God.

4) Giving more than receiving. Children want only to receive. A sign of maturity is a growing enjoyment in giving more than receiving.

5) Practicing consistency, helpfulness, and mutual satisfaction. Getting along with others, being part of the solution instead of the problem, and other personal relationship skills are characteristics of the mature person.

6) Redirect anger toward constructive ends. Anger creates adrenaline (energy) which must be released. Mature people release it in positive instead of negative ways.

2. Pray for the progress of their love. "Increase and abound in love to one another" (verse 12). Note the progression in love: Increase; increase and abound; increase and abound toward one another; increase and abound toward all. Love originates in one heart but should end up impacting all who are near. We should pray that new believers learn to let their love abound to those who have not experienced the love found in the Gospel of Christ.

3. Pray for the purity of their lives. "So that He may establish your hearts blameless in holiness before our God and Father at the coming of our Lord Jesus Christ with all His saints" (verse 13). The ultimate purpose of all prayer for new believers is that they might persevere in faith, blameless and holy, until the second coming of Christ.

May I encourage you to lead some to Christ—then pray for them to be faithful and protected from the attack of the Enemy; that they might be perfected in their faith.

APPLICATION

1. How does Hebrews 11:1 describe faith?

2. What do you learn about the basic elements of faith from the following verses:

   a. Genesis 15:6

   b. Proverbs 3:5

   c. Romans 3:22

3. What do you learn about the truths on which faith is based from the following verses?

   a. I Timothy 3:9

   b. I Timothy 4:1

   c. II Timothy 3:16

   d. Jude 3

Growing Up in Your Faith

4. Read Matthew 13:18–23.

    a. What is the first thing that can happen to a new believer? (verse 19)

    b. What is a second thing that can happen to a new believer? (verses 20–21)

    c. What is a third thing that can happen to a new believer? (verse 22)

    d. What is the ideal thing to happen to a new believer? (verse 23)

    e. What do you think makes the difference in whether a new believer bears fruit a hundred, sixty, or thirty times what was sown? (verse 24)

5. Read Hebrews 12:4–13.

    a. What are two attitudinal temptations when we undergo hardship? (verse 5)

b. Why should we not be bitter or discouraged if we know that hardship is from the Lord?

c. If you are loved by God, what can you expect to experience? (verse 6)

d. If you never experience chastening from the Lord, what does that suggest? (verse 8)

e. What is the expected response of a son to the choices of his father? (verse 9)

f. Why does God allow us to undergo hardship? (verse 10)

f. If you don't respond submissively to hardship, what will you not partake of? (verse 10)

g. Contrast the "during" and "after" of hardship: (verse 11)

h. What kinds of preparation should you make for enduring hardship? (verses 12–13)

6. Read Galatians 1:6–10.

   a. What were the new believers in Galatia contemplating doing? (verse 6)

   b. How did Paul feel about those who were trying to pervert their faith? (verse 8)

   c. Who was Paul more concerned about offending by his stance? (verse 10)

7. What was the biggest temptation or hardship you faced as a new believer in Christ? What do you wish someone had done for you?

DID YOU KNOW?

The Apostle Paul was a man whose mind stayed on others more than himself. While Paul no doubt prayed for himself, and even asked others to do so on his behalf (Romans 15:30–32; Ephesians 6:19–20), no fewer than 42 instances of prayers of thanksgiving or intercession for others are found in Paul's 13 epistles. No wonder the churches he founded prospered and grew.

LESSON 7

THE CALL TO A HOLY LIFE

I Thessalonians 4:1–12

In this lesson we discover what it means for the Christian to be holy.

OUTLINE

A holy person has often been thought of as strict, somber, suspicious, and staying on the straight and narrow. While those could be admirable traits in the right setting, altogether they represent a caricature of holiness, not the real thing. A holy person is simply one committed to obeying God.

I. **The Meaning of a Holy Life**
   A. A Holy Life Is a Life That Pleases God
   B. A Holy Life Is a Life of Progress with God
   C. A Holy Life Is a Life of Purity
   D. A Holy Life Is a Life of Personal Control over Your Body
   E. A Holy Life Is a Powerfully Transformed Life
   F. A Holy Life Is a Practical Life

II. **The Motives for a Holy Life**
   A. God Commands Us to Be Holy
   B. My Christian Growth Calls Me to Be Holy
   C. The World That Watches Compels Me to Be Holy

III. **The Method of a Holy Life**

OVERVIEW

As a result of working through cancer treatments and being restored to health by God's good favor, an interesting proposition was presented to me in the community where I live: Would I join a Jewish rabbi, who is also a cancer survivor, and talk in a public setting about the role my faith played in my bout with cancer? Being a bit hesitant at first, I finally decided to accept the invitation and pray God would give me an unfettered opportunity to speak publicly of my faith in Christ—which He did.

While I have come to appreciate very much on a personal level the Jewish rabbi who spoke, I quickly discovered that we were coming from radically different perspectives concerning God and His role in our lives. He believes very few things that I believe about God—and not just regarding Christ, but regarding eternal life, prayer, God's sovereignty, and other matters which are the foundations of the Christian faith.

If I could summarize the differences in his approach and mine, it would be to say that my views are anchored firmly in the Bible while he feels the freedom to adjust his views about God based on his changing personal standards or cultural mores. That is, of course, not uncommon for "religious" folk who have no standard or authoritative source in which to anchor their faith. But it also represents a danger for Christians. We can redefine God to fit our own idea of what He should be like if we do not stay focused on knowing Him as we find Him in the Word of God.

In I Thessalonians 4:1–12 Paul focuses on the importance of holiness, especially abstaining from sexual immorality and uncleanness. Christians who follow the rabbi's approach to standards can justify redefining what God says about these concepts in light of our culture's permissive attitudes toward immorality. They can redefine who God is and what He says to the point that an immoral lifestyle is no longer immoral.

But God does not change. The fundamental attribute of His character and nature is holiness. To redefine His character by focusing on love and acceptance instead of holiness is a fundamental error, for we will see that God's love flows from His holiness. Cultures and their standards come and go, but God does not change. The verses we will study in this lesson are very important for the church today—to be reminded of who God is and what He expects of us.

In the last verse of chapter three we find Paul longing that the Thessalonians' hearts would be established blameless in holiness. He expands on that desire in chapter four, focusing on the sanctification that must flow from right faith and doctrine. The doctrine in which Paul had established the church in Thessalonica must now translate itself into holy living.

In chapter four we will find Paul discussing three different kinds of sanctification (or holiness): Positional (4:7), progressive (4:3), and perfect (3:13; 4:13–18). These three actually represent three different "tenses" of salvation. We were saved in the past (positional sanctification), we are being saved in the present (progressive sanctification), and we will be forever saved in the future (perfect sanctification). Understanding these three in more detail will provide needed background to Paul's teaching:

1. Positional Sanctification. Verse 7 speaks of a time in the past when God called us to a position of holiness. When we are saved, we are set apart unto Jesus Christ, though we are not completely holy in our behavior (I Corinthians 1:30). Positionally, we are in Christ and are viewed as holy by God. Positionally speaking, when God sees the Christian He does not see us and our sin, but sees us in our standing in Christ.

2. Progressive Sanctification. Verse 3 is an example of the challenge of progressive sanctification, conforming ourselves daily to God's standards of holiness in our behavior. Though we are positioned in Christ from God's perspective, while we are on this earth we are still in our sins. No one is perfectly sanctified experientially this side of heaven (though some cults have sprung up around the error of "sinless perfection"). Positional sanctification we can call justification; progressive sanctification is what we normally refer to as sanctification; and perfect sanctification we can call glorification. We are to live every day in light of what we have been (justified) and what we will be (glorified).

3. Perfect Sanctification. The last verse of chapter three (3:13) is where perfect sanctification is first mentioned, though Paul takes it up again in 4:13–18. This sanctification is the holiness we will experience at the Rapture of the church when we are changed immediately into a perfect state of sinlessness for all eternity.

In chapter four, we have an outline of the three types of sanctification. It was planned by God (4:1–8), it should be practiced by believers (4:9–12), and it will be perfected at the Rapture (4:13–17). The idea that we could somehow redefine God's standard of holiness to make it match our expectations is totally out of bounds. Holiness is God's will—it always has been, it is now, and always will be.

The Bible makes us uncomfortable at times, which is good. It's easy to get casual about God, to think of Him as someone who understands our weaknesses and looks the other way. He does know we're sinners, and He does understand our weaknesses, but He does not look the other way. Why would the Scriptures be full of exhortations to be holy if God did not expect us to comply? But He does not leave us on our own to become holy. He sets the standard and then equips us to meet it.

The Meaning of a Holy Life

Paul says in verse three that sanctification is the will of God for us, and in verse seven that God called us to holiness. Therefore, we need to know the marks of a holy life.

A Holy Life Is a Life That Pleases God

The only life that pleases God is a holy life (4:1b). And that, at the most basic level, is a morally pure life. We shouldn't try to make this more complicated than necessary. Most people don't need an explanation of what a clean life is. Lest we fall in the category of "ignorant brethren" (Romans 11:25; I Corinthians 12:1; II Corinthians 1:8; I Thessalonians 4:13), Paul makes it very clear that to be holy means, for example, to "abstain from sexual immorality" (4:3) among other things. The issue is not whether we are as bad as someone else or better than we used to be. The issue is what does God say about being holy—and are we measuring up to His standard? We do not change God or His standards in order to bring Him down to our level of "holiness." Rather, we conform our lives to Him.

A Holy Life Is a Life of Progress with God

When Paul exhorts us in verse one to "abound more and more," he is letting us know that we never arrive in our pursuit of holiness. There is no plateau in the Christian life, no mountain peak at which we can cease from our efforts to be holy. Whenever we get to a point in the Christian life where we think we've made a measure of progress, we suddenly realize how much more we don't know, how much further we have to go.

I used to worry about the fact that I always seemed to feel dissatisfied in my walk with Christ because I knew I wasn't where I should be and wanted to be. I was frustrated at never being able to attain what I thought was the goal. But now I understand that those are the feelings of anyone who is making progress in holiness. The edge you feel, the gap between where you are and where you want to be, is what keeps us "abounding more and more." And so I continue on, striving to become all I can for Christ, knowing that He who began a good work in me (justification) will complete it (sanctification) until the day of Christ Jesus (glorification) (Philippians 1:6).

God is at work in every believer. Progress, not perfection, is the goal. We will never be perfectly holy in this life, but faithful progress to submit every area of life to the Lord is what will cause us to "abound more and more" every day.

A Holy Life Is a Life of Purity

Paul does not mince words: It is God's will that all believers abstain from sexual immorality (4:3). The apostle focused on this in his letter because sexual immorality was a serious problem in pagan cultures of the first century. And unfortunately, it is a serious problem in our day as well. So the letter applies perfectly to us. Sadly, sexual immorality is an accepted part of the religious landscape in many churches today.

This is an example of conforming God's standards of holiness to our own emotional and physical desires. If that is what we are going to do, why do we even need God? The whole purpose for God redeeming us is to lift us up out of the miry clay we were bogged down in because of our sin. It makes no sense to say we embrace the God of the Bible and then say it is His will for us to live in that which He came to save us from.

There are two areas of impurity from which the Christian is to abstain:

1. We are to abstain from moral impurity. Verses 4–6 could not be clearer as to what Paul means. It is not surprising for him to be so explicit with new Christians such as those in Thessalonica for whom total abstinence from sexually immoral practices might have come as a shock. It is surprising, however, to consider that the church in America is still in need of those same explicit instructions. The Thessalonians were hearing these standards for the first

time while we have had access to Paul's words for more than 1,900 years.

Our church staff recently completed the laborious process of putting together a position paper on the subjects of divorce, remarriage, and church discipline. It is an unfortunate reality that we need those guidelines in our day, but we do. We have individuals in our church who are being subjected to church discipline because they do not choose to comply with God's standards of holiness regarding sexual immorality and the defrauding of a brother. You can not do that and maintain fellowship with the body of Christ as if nothing is wrong. People who choose to live in immorality and will not repent are put out of the church. This is a difficult decision for any church to make, but it must be made. God's standards are not ours to redefine.

Again, the issue is not perfection, it is confession and repentance. When you sin, what do you do about it?

Another of God's standards is forgiveness, and we practice that as carefully as we practice the standard of holiness leading to discipline. We would be just as wrong not to welcome a repentant sinner as we would not to put out of the church the unrepentant one. Holiness requires that we keep God's standards both ways. But even if the church makes a mistake in its best efforts to discern the details and justice of a particular situation, God's justice will still be served. "The Lord is the avenger of all such" as have been defrauded by a brother (4:6). He will keep His standards and avenge the one who has been hurt even if the church misses its cue and fails to do so. God is the one who oversees His own standards. A sin against holiness is a sin against God.

2. We are to abstain from mental impurity. The "passion of lust" Paul mentions in verse 5 has to do with the indecency of the mind. Lustful thoughts, incestuous affections, fleshly carnality, pornography, Internet sex—the list goes on and on of things which fall into the category of mental impurity. All of those sins are violations of God's standards of holiness. And the opportunities to participate in them are everywhere in our world—even more so than in Paul's time. We should not live like the ungodly who avail themselves of any and every opportunity for impurity. We should live holy lives.

A Holy Life Is a Life of Personal Control over Your Body

Paul says each Christian is responsible for keeping his or her body under control—and this applies to both men and women. Each Christian is the temple of the Holy Spirit (I Corinthians 6:19–20) and should not offer up his or her body as a vehicle or instrument of unrighteousness (Romans 6:13).

I believe this standard has to do with all areas of our physical appetites—not just sex. We live in a day when more people are obese and dying of diet-related diseases than at any time in our history. Gluttony and lack of self control at the dinner table are not holy practices.

A Holy Life Is a Powerfully Transformed Life

If we are truly born again people, our behavior should reflect a change. We are not to live like the people we used to be; like those "who do not know God" (4:5). Paul's point is that if we live unholy lives we may as well hang a sign on our back that says our Christianity is not genuine. Pagans live unholy lives, not Christians. So if we live like pagans we call into question the very essence of our conversion to Christ. That's not to say there aren't some moral, upright people who aren't Christians. But with reference to the entire scheme of the pagan way of life, where there are no standards for personal holiness—that is what we are no longer to be like.

A Holy Life Is a Practical Life

Many people, even some Christians, wonder if it is possible, not to mention practical, to live a holy life today. It is possible and practical because God would not expect it of us if it weren't. A holy life is a life of humility and honesty.

1. A holy life is a life of humility

    Paul says in verse 11 that a holy life will be found to be a quiet, humble life. Holy people "mind [their] own business" (4:11). That phrase doesn't mean exactly what we take it to mean in our day. It basically meant to take care of your financial affairs, to keep your life in order so that your life was not a disruption to others. I meet people all the time who have come out of churches which split because someone was intent on causing trouble. We are to live humble lives,

keeping our affairs in order, working to meet our own needs (4:11–12).
2. A holy life is a life of honesty

A holy person is a person who walks a transparent life. He is honest and has integrity. He pays his debts and keeps his promises. He isn't a troublemaker but a person whose life reflects a peaceful and honest approach—nothing to hide, everything up front, no ulterior motives. A holy person is a person you feel comfortable being around.

THE MOTIVES FOR A HOLY LIFE

What specific reasons can we identify for maintaining a life of holiness? We agree that the standards are high—so what is our motivation for keeping them?

God Commands Us to Be Holy

God's will is the first and foremost reason. It is not being simplistic to say that because God says so is the best reason for doing anything. It really is the best reason! What better reason could we offer? He tells us to pray, to worship, to give, to love, to serve, to forgive—and we do all of those things because He tells us to. In chapter four, note how many times holiness is attached to the Lord Himself, proving that this really is something important to Him: We are exhorted to do this "in the Lord Jesus" (4:1); the command to be holy comes "through the Lord Jesus" (4:2); holiness is "the will of God" (4:3); God calls us to holiness (4:7); to reject holiness is to reject God (4:8).

As mentioned earlier, holiness is the chief attribute of God. If there is any one thing God would expect us to do in imitating Him, it is to be holy. Being obedient to God is a worthy motive for being holy.

My Christian Growth Calls Me to Be Holy

No Christian can grow spiritually apart from being holy; it is the key to growing in grace. Because we grow as believers by the grace of God and the power of the Holy Spirit, we must be holy to avail ourselves of those agencies of growth. We cannot be immoral or impure and expect the Holy Spirit to manifest His fruit through us. We should echo the prayer of the 19th century Scottish pastor, Robert Murray McCheyne: "Lord God, make me as holy as it is possible for a redeemed sinner to be."

The World That Watches Compels Me to Be Holy

Verse 12 says, "That you may walk properly toward those who are outside" (see also Colossians 4:5; I Timothy 3:7). Truth be told, the world has greater expectations of Christians than we realize. If a non-Christian knows you are a Christian, he doesn't expect you to live like the rest of the world. He expects you to be better (holy). Why do you think phrases like, "I thought you were a Christian!" or, "And you call yourself a Christian!" are used so often? The world may not agree with the Christian lifestyle, but they know what it is and expect Christians to follow it. That's why it is so hurtful to the cause of Christ when churches have disruptive splits and Christians, especially leaders, fall into immorality. The world knows we're not supposed to act like that.

Christians and their leaders don't even have to cross over the line of immorality—we just have to get near it—for the world and its media outlets to be all over it. Of course, their intent is to discredit the cause of Christ and point out the hypocrisy of Christians. And if there has genuinely been sin involved, then they have every right to call us on the carpet. Because we are not supposed to sin; we are to live holy lives. Satan delights in Christians who fail to be holy. He will make the way smooth and easy for us to walk right into temptation if possible so as to discredit the name of Christ and bring reproach on the Gospel. The possibility of any Christian sinning, even being tempted to get near the line dividing holiness from impurity, is real. I have to warn myself as I warn you to be on guard, to be vigilant and watchful. One impure thought can lead to an impure act and bring shame on the Savior.

THE METHOD OF A HOLY LIFE

It has been well said that the Christian life is not a difficult life—it's an impossible life. That's why Paul was being such an encouragement to the Thessalonian Christians. In chapter 3, verses 12 and 13, he prayed through his letter that the Lord would allow the Thessalonians to increase in their maturity, to be established "blameless in holiness before our God and Father at the coming of our Lord Jesus Christ with all His saints." And in verse 10 he says he's been praying for them, and the opportunity to minister to them again, "night and day." Having people pray for you to be holy is essential.

But the Holy Spirit is also essential. To reject the message of holiness is to reject God who has given us the Holy Spirit—notice, the Spirit is the *Holy* Spirit (4:8). A holy person is a person who manifests the fruit of the Spirit, the very attributes and characteristics of Jesus Christ Himself (Galatians 5:22–23). We need to be filled with the Holy Spirit every day (Ephesians 5:18). We need to confess our sins quickly and rid our lives of impure thoughts and actions. And the Spirit of God is the One who is called alongside us to encourage us to do that—to encourage us and lead us into holiness.

God has not changed and holiness has not changed. There is no less a need for holiness in the 21st century than in the first century, and no less an expectation of holiness by God. We will not wish the standards of holiness away by our desires for them to be less stringent. As Christians, our only response is . . . to be holy as He is holy (Leviticus 11:45).

APPLICATION

1. Read I Corinthians 6:9–11.

   a. List all the unholy behaviors Paul describes in verses 9–10:

   b. What does Paul say about their future? (verses 9a, 10b)

   c. What had the Corinthians been prior to becoming Christians? (verse 11a)

   d. What does Paul's use of the past tense "were" imply? (verse 11a)

   e. What three action words does Paul use in verse 11 to describe what happened to the Corinthians?

   f. Who performed the action? (verse 11b)

   g. What did the Corinthians need to be "washed" clean of? (verse 11)

The Call to a Holy Life • 105

h. What does "sanctified" in this context mean? (verse 11)

i. What does "justified" mean? (verse 11)

j. Is the sanctification Paul refers to here positional, progressive, or permanent?

l. Explain how a person can be a "fornicator" (verse 9) one minute and be sanctified (holy; verse 11) the next minute:

m. Were you sanctified when you became a Christian? In what sense? (positionally, experientially, or forever)

2. What simple definition of holiness can you glean from I Corinthians 7:34?

   a. Why did God choose people before the foundation of the world to be believers in Christ? (Ephesians 1:4)

b. What synonym for holy do you find in Ephesians 5:27?

3. Read I Peter 1:13–16.
   a. What three things does Peter exhort believers to do in verse 13?

   b. What is the goal of such actions? (verse 14)

   c. What does "obedience" suggest about the believer's responsibility in these actions? (verse 14)

   d. At what stage of life were believers ignorant? (verse 14)

   e. If Christians are not conformed to the former lusts (verse 14), what will they be? (verse 15)

   f. What is the fundamental reason Christians are to be holy? (verse 16)

g. I Peter 1:16 is a quote from Leviticus 11:44–45. What was the original setting of this statement? (Leviticus 11:1–47, esp. verses 46–47).

h. Why was holiness the issue in a discussion of clean and unclean animals?

i. What does that tell you about the original meaning of "holiness?"

j. How does this passage help you understand the requirements for holiness (set-apartness) in II Corinthians 6:14–18?

DID YOU KNOW?

"Holy" originally was used in Scripture in a different sense than we're used to thinking of. For instance, dirt was holy. And temple prostitutes were holy. How could a word we equate with "squeaky clean" be used to describe dirt and immoral people? Simply because the root meaning of "holy" was "set apart." If something were set apart or designated for a special use, it was holy. That's why dirt that was not holy one minute was holy the next—because it was set apart by God as the place where Moses would meet with Him (Exodus 3:5). "Set apart" is still a good definition for holy since saints ("holy ones") have been set aside by God for His purposes (I Corinthians 1:2).

LESSON 8

THE RAPTURE OF THE CHURCH

I Thessalonians 4:13–18

In this lesson we learn how and why the church will be removed from earth.

OUTLINE

Most people don't regard funerals as settings of hope—but they should be if the deceased were a Christian. Death has no permanent hold on the believer. One day every person who has died in Christ will come out of his grave to meet the Lord—and their believing loved ones—in the clouds.

I. **The Careful Preview of the Rapture**
   A. Dispelling the Believers' Ignorance
   B. Describing the Believers' Death

II. **The Certain Promise of the Rapture**

III. **The Chronological Program of the Rapture**
   A. The Return
   B. The Resurrection
   C. The Rapture
   D. The Reunion

IV. **The Comforting Purpose of the Rapture**

OVERVIEW

Prior to April, 1996, you could have announced you were going to speak on the Rapture of the church and most Americans would have reacted quizzically—even some Christians. But authors Tim Lahaye and Jerry Jenkins have helped to remedy that situation with their *Left Behind* series of books on the end times. At this moment, more than 20 million copies of the first nine volumes in the series have been published, volume one dealing specifically with the Rapture of the church. In addition, volume one, titled *Left Behind*, has been made into a major motion picture. As a result, if you mention the Rapture of the church in 2001, a lot more people in America know what you are talking about.

The Rapture of the church is part one of a two-stage series of events surrounding the second coming of Jesus Christ to earth. Many passages in the Old Testament (like Zechariah 14:1–5) foresaw Jesus' coming with power as the Son of Man to reign and rule over all the earth. According to Revelation 1:7, that second part of His coming will be a public event, seen by everyone. It will take place in the clouds, all of His saints will be with Him, and everyone will see Him. The purpose of that coming is for Christ to establish His throne in Jerusalem and to judge those who have rejected the grace of God on earth (II Thessalonians 1:7–8).

But Christ coming as judge is the second part of His coming. The first stage of His return is what we will study in this lesson, the Rapture of the Church. That is the moment at which Christ comes to receive His Church to Himself, to remove them from the earth before His judgment begins. The Rapture of the Church is the fulfillment of the promise Christ made to His disciples in John 14: "And if I go and prepare a place for you, I will come again and receive you to Myself; that where I am, there you may be also" (verse 3). At this point on God's prophetic timetable, the Rapture of the Church is the next major event. It could occur at any moment, and for that reason is often referred to as "imminent."

Two key passages in the New Testament teach about the Rapture of the Church. Besides the passage we will study in this lesson, the other is I Corinthians 15. But even with these two passages to work from, the church has not agreed on the specifics concerning the Rapture. There is agreement that Christ will return to earth a second time, but disagreement on the order of events, and specifically on the timing and nature of the Rapture.

The reason the topic comes up in I Thessalonians is because the believers there were new in the faith and had not been instructed on such matters; they were being persecuted and were discouraged; and they were confused about the state of some who might die before Christ returned. So, in I Thessalonians Paul assures them that no saint, dead or alive, is going to miss the Rapture. And in II Thessalonians he assures them no saint will go through the Tribulation, or the time of judgment to be executed by Christ just prior to His Second Coming.

While there is disagreement on the timing of the Rapture (and we will look at more details of that in the next lesson), suffice it to say at this juncture that the purpose of the Rapture is to spare the Church from the Tribulation. The Bible says there is no condemnation for those who are in Christ Jesus (Romans 8:1), and that includes the Tribulation condemnation God will bring upon those who have rejected His offer of salvation. It is my clear understanding of Scripture that the Christians for whom Christ suffered and died, will not suffer through the judgments of the Tribulation period.

It is natural, even today, for many questions to be raised concerning this subject, and especially concerning those who will not be alive at the time Christ comes in the clouds to gather the Church to Himself. What about them? That is the specific focus of Paul's teaching in I Thessalonians 4. And I confess—as often as I have studied this passage of Scripture, I am still greatly intrigued about how it is all going to work out. Anyone who has relatives or ancestors who died as believers in Christ has a stake in understanding as much as they can about the events Paul describes.

The English word "rapture" is not found in Scripture; the term is used to describe the events of II Thessalonians 4:17—a catching up of the saints. While "rapture" actually derives from the Latin translation of verse 17, it is ironic that the word means joy or ecstasy in English. It reminds us that the Rapture of the Church is going to be a moment of unparalleled joy and spiritual ecstasy as believers are transported from earth to the heavenlies and the presence of Christ.

THE CAREFUL PREVIEW OF THE RAPTURE (4:13–14)

The first thing Paul wants to do in dealing with the Rapture is to dispel the ignorance of the believers in Thessalonica.

Dispelling the Believers' Ignorance

Someone was once asked, "What is the largest denomination in all of the world?" And the answer was "The Ignorant Brethren." That's obviously not a verifiable answer, but Paul does say frequently in the New Testament that his purpose is to do away with ignorance (Romans 11:25; I Corinthians 12:1; II Corinthians 1:8). He said it because the believers were . . . ignorant! That's not a derogatory term, it's just a fact. They don't yet know the truth about that which was a concern to them. And he didn't want them to remain in a state of ignorance and confusion—especially concerning those who had "fallen asleep," or died. Instead of living in despair, Paul wanted them to live in hope.

Describing the Believers' Death

The "sleep" Paul is talking about comes from the Greek word *koimao*. In the New Testament, *koimao* does not mean sleep in the normal sense. Rather, it has a metaphorical meaning of death. It is used that way by John in referring to Jesus' words about Lazarus who had died (John 11:11). And it is used to describe Stephen when he died as a result of stoning by the Jews (Acts 7:60). When Paul refers to the death of king David, he says he "fell asleep" (Acts 13:36), as well as when he refers to those who witnessed the resurrected Christ but are now dead (I Corinthians 15:6). He also, in I Corinthians, refers to believers who have died as having "fallen asleep" (I Corinthians 15:18, 20).

It is understandable that, for Christians, the concept of death should be likened to sleep since the expectation was that we would be awakened (resurrected from the dead) one day when Christ returns. Our modern word "cemetery" is taken from the Greek word *koimeteria*, which was a place for burying the dead—a "sleeping place." The word was also used for an inn, a place where travelers could sleep temporarily. The expectation was that you would get up and continue your journey after a brief period of rest, just as it is today with our hotels and motels. When Christians die, their souls and spirits go immediately to be with the Lord. The bodies of Christians who die are "asleep" until the coming of the Lord. At that time, their bodies will be "awakened" and united with their souls and spirits. It is important to understand that the Greek word is never used for the sleep of the soul—only the body. The believer's soul is continually awake in the presence of the Lord until the body of the believer is raised from the dead.

Paul's words are a reminder of what a wonderful hope we have—that death is not a permanent event. That is why he compares the believer with those who sorrow, those who have no such hope of life after death. The Christian has a hope which no other person in the world has. No other religion offers the great and precious promise of life after death that Christianity does. When the Christian stands beside the grave of a loved one, he knows he will see that loved one again. We sorrow naturally at the death of a loved one since we will miss their company and presence. But we do not sorrow "as others who have no hope" (4:13). The tears I shed at my own parents' funerals were real—I miss their fellowship and the comfort of their presence. But I did not cry tears of despair for I know I will see them again soon.

This passage is a great commentary on I Corinthians 15 where Paul says that Christ has taken the sting out of death (verses 55–56) for the Christian. The sting Christ removed is the idea that death is the end; that there is nothing more to "life" after death. He changed death from death to "sleep;" He made death just a temporary aside until we are resurrected and begin to enjoy the eternal life we received when we became a Christian.

So, Paul tells the Thessalonian believers, the deceased have not been excluded from the Rapture. They will be there as surely as those who are alive when Christ comes for the Church. Dispelling whatever false information the believers had been given must have brought great joy to them—as it does to us.

THE CERTAIN PROMISE OF THE RAPTURE (4:15)

Paul summarizes verses 13 and 14 with a clear promise: "We who are alive and remain until the coming of the Lord will by no means precede those who are asleep." And this is not just Paul's opinion. What he says he promises "by the word of the Lord." Here's what I think Paul means by this reference to authority. The Rapture of the Church is not mentioned in the four gospels, nor will you find reference to it in the Old Testament. It is not until we get to Paul's writing that we find the Rapture discussed. And that is because Paul got it as a direct revelation from the Lord—the revelation of a "mystery," as he calls the Rapture in I Corinthians 15:51.

Not only do the dead rise at the Rapture, they rise first. If we who are living don't precede them, then they precede us. The dead are first in time and in prominence, according to the use of *protas* ("first") in verse 16. So those believers who have lost loved ones in the Lord will see them rise first to meet Christ in the air. They take the prominent place.

So, we have learned from Paul so far that the Rapture is not just for the living, it is for all who are in Christ—deceased or alive. Second, we have learned that the dead in Christ will rise first, followed by those who are living at the time of the Rapture. Now, what about the timing of the events which make up this grand reunion for believers with each other and with their Lord?

THE CHRONOLOGICAL PROGRAM OF THE RAPTURE (4:16-17))

Four key events are specifically described by Paul in the order in which they will occur:

The Return (verse 16)

Verse 16 says, "For the Lord Himself will descend from heaven with a shout, with the voice of an archangel, and with the trumpet of God." When the Lord comes in judgment He sends His angels as reaping ministers, but at the Rapture "the Lord Himself" comes. That is in keeping with what the angels told the apostles at Christ's resurrection: "This same Jesus . . . will so come in like manner . . ." (Acts 1:11). Not the angels, not the Holy Spirit, but the Lord Jesus Himself descends from heaven and catches up the Church to Himself.

There will be sounds accompanying His appearing: a shout, the voice of an archangel, and the trumpet of God. But these are not three distinct and different sounds occurring one after another. There is only one sound at the appearing of Christ and it is described by Paul in three different ways. The passage could be read this way: "The Lord shall descend with a shout which is like such a thing as the voice of an archangel and such a thing as a trumpet of God." No one knows what it will sound like, but it will likely be like nothing ever heard on earth before. As such, it will be instantly recognizable by those who belong to the Lord.

The Resurrection (verse 16)

Paul continues, "And the dead in Christ will rise first." There is another resurrection coming later where non-believers will be raised—and you don't want to be involved in that resurrection

(Revelation 20:5, 11–15). If you are not alive at the Rapture, when Christ returns for the Church, then you want to be raised in this resurrection to meet Him in the air. William Barclay, a commentator on the New Testament books, wrote some wonderful words about this resurrection:

"If a man has lived in Christ, and died in Christ, even if he is dead, he is still in Christ. That means that between Jesus Christ and the man who loves him, there is a relationship which nothing can break. It is a relationship which overpasses death. Because Jesus Christ lived and died and rose again, so the man in Christ shall live and die and rise again. Nothing in life or death can ever separate him from Christ."

The person who has died in Christ, and the person who is alive in Christ, will enjoy the same blessed reunion with Christ. The resurrection is the great hope of every believer who dies before Christ returns.

The Rapture (verse 17)

Paul continues, "Then we who are alive and remain shall be caught up together with them in the clouds to meet the Lord in the air. . . ." The words "caught up" are what we refer to by the word "rapture." The Greek word, *harpazo,* has several interesting meanings:

1. To carry off by force

   The word can mean to forcefully remove or carry off, and it has significant meaning for the Rapture. Satan and his minions will do whatever they can to block the uniting of Christ with His Church, but the Lord will overpower the Enemy and remove believers "by force."

2. To claim for oneself eagerly

   Another of the word's meanings implies the eagerness with which Christ will return to embrace those who are His, those He redeemed by His own shed blood.

3. To snatch away speedily

   This meaning refers to the sudden nature of the Rapture. Paul says in I Corinthians 15:52 that the Rapture will take place "in a moment, in the twinkling of an eye, at the last trumpet." We are going to be translated from earth to heaven in a mere moment. It will be an event that will astonish the rest of the world—millions of believing Christians will simply vanish off the face of the earth.

4. To rescue from the danger of destruction

    This may be the most important meaning of the four from the perspective of God's plan for planet earth. Believers will be removed from the earth before the judgment of the Tribulation takes place and many, many unbelievers are destroyed.

Some wonder at the unusual nature of this event—believers being suddenly removed from earth. But it has happened before. In Hebrews 11:5 we read of Enoch whom God took from earth before he died (Genesis 5:24). Then there was Elijah who went up "by a whirlwind into heaven" (II Kings 2:11). An instance we don't often think about in this regard is Paul himself who was "caught up to the third heaven . . . caught up into Paradise" (II Corinthians 12:2, 4). Twice Paul uses the same word, *harpazo*, to describe his own experience. Of course, Paul didn't remain in heaven, but he got there the same way we will get there— by being snatched away in a moment of time.

The Reunion (verse 17)

The reunion occurs when the dead and the living in Christ meet one another and together meet the Lord in the air: "Then we who are alive and remain shall be caught up together with them in the clouds to meet the Lord in their air. And thus we shall always be with the Lord." Let's be clear about what takes place at this reunion. The real person, the soul and spirit of a Christian, leaves the body at death and goes into the presence of the Lord. So when the dead are raised, the living person who has been in the presence of Christ is reunited with their glorified, resurrected body. That's the first part of the reunion.

Then, resurrected believers are going to meet the living believers in the air. They rise before the living do, but we all meet in the air. That means we all proceed to meet the Lord together in the air. I have thought about what a great time of fellowship and joy that reunion will be. If you're like me, you don't like to watch something beautiful or meaningful or exciting by yourself. As much as I love to watch football on television, I'd much rather watch it with my wife and kids than by myself. It's just more fun to get excited with others who are as excited as you are. That's the way the Rapture is going to be. We are going to be with those we are closest to in the Lord enjoying the most exciting event in history!

In biblical days, when a person of importance would visit the ruler of a distant city, the ruler would send a royal ambassador and his entourage out of the city to greet the visitors and escort them back into the city. That is exactly how we come into the presence of God. We will be greeted by the Lord Jesus Christ Himself and escorted into heaven. How could anyone who knows about the glory of that day not want to become a Christian and be a part of it.

THE COMFORTING PURPOSE OF THE RAPTURE (4:18)

We know the effect that a lack of knowledge must have had on the Thessalonian Christians, for in verse 18 he encourages them to "comfort one another with these words." They must have been genuinely in despair over the state of their deceased loved ones who had not remained alive until the coming of the Lord.

I can't count the number of times as a pastor I have stood at the graveside of a deceased believer and comforted the family with Paul's words. And what a comfort they are! It is not easy to say good-bye to a loved one, even under the best of circumstances. And if there is any comfort at all to be taken in those times, it is in the fact that we will see that person again. Remember this wonderful verse the next time you need to extend a word of grace to one who has lost a loved one. Let them know that at the Rapture of the Church that one who has just died will come out of the ground, join the Lord to return to heaven, never to be separated from their loved ones again. If you can, read it to them from the Bible so they'll know you aren't making it up. You'd be surprised how many Christians do not know the truth about the Rapture—what will happen one day to the dead in Christ.

Paul often exhorts believers to comfort each other with the words of truth he has written. It happens again with the Thessalonians in chapter 5, verse 11, after he has instructed them regarding the Day of the Lord, another aspect of end-time truth. These verses of comfort in I Thessalonians are a stern rebuke to those who say prophecy has no real practical value. Whenever I hear that, I know I have met a member of "The Ignorant Brethren" denomination. The great purpose in all prophetic texts is to give hope to the believer; to let the believer know that God has a plan and a purpose in the future. When you are suffering, either for the sake of the Gospel as the Thessalonians were, or for any reason, it is a great comfort to know that heaven awaits you. And if you've been separated from loved ones by death, the same reality applies. This life is not all there is! We look for the day when we will be united with the rest of the Church and our Lord Jesus Christ. If that is not a comfort, what could be?

Two applications flow naturally from this great passage of Scripture. First, be looking for the Lord. As already stated, the Rapture of the Church is the next event on God's prophetic agenda. It could happen before you finish reading this lesson. Are you ready? Second, be living for the Lord. Just because we know the Lord could return at any moment is no reason to fold our hands and wait. I want to be found abounding in the work of the Lord when He returns (I Corinthians 15:58), not relaxing in the midst of a perishing world.

Please join me today in looking and living for the Lord who is soon to appear in the clouds. What a day that will be!

APPLICATION

1. Read Zechariah 14:1–7.

    a. What is the topic of this passage? (verse 1a)

    b. What will the nations do in that "day?" (verse 2)

    c. What will the Lord do to defend Jerusalem? (verse 3)

    d. What dramatic event will take place in Jerusalem? (verse 4)

    e. What role will the saints of God play? (verse 5)

f. What phenomenon will occur in the heavens? (verse 6)

g. Note as many differences/similarities as you can between this event and the event Paul describes in I Thessalonians 4:13–18 (location, key figures, the role of the saints, etc.):

h. What is your conclusion? Are the two passages describing the same or different events?

2. Read John 14:1–4.

   a. What parallel do you find in verse 1 with I Thessalonians 4:18?

b. How is Proverbs 3:5–6 a good parallel for John 14:1b when it comes to understanding all the details of the future?

c. Read "I go to prepare a place for you" (verses 2–3) in light of Exodus 23:20–24. Who might the Angel have been who was guiding Israel into her prepared place?

d. Does verse 3 sound more like Zechariah 14:1–7 or I Thessalonians 4:13–18?

e. How might Christ's role as the One who goes ahead of you give you encouragement in dealing with unknown issues in your life?

f. At this moment, what does Christ have prepared for you in heaven? (verse 3)

g. What do you think could prevent you from occupying that place one day?

h. Who do you know who has no place in heaven prepared for them for eternity?

i. What could you do for them which might help their hearts not to be troubled? (verse 1)

3. Read I Corinthians 15:12–58

   a. How serious is the fact of Christ's resurrection to the Christian? (verse 14)

   b. If Christ wasn't raised from the dead, what chance does the Christian have of being resurrected?

c. What would you say to a person who says he's a Christian but also says the resurrection is not a "critical" doctrine and may never have happened? (verse 17)

d. What would you say to a person who believes the emphasis of the Christian life should be on the here and now, not "pie in the sky?" (verse 19)

e. Why is Christ called "the firstfruits" in verse 23?

f. Besides uniting us with Christ, what role does the transformation at the Rapture play? (verses 50–52)

g. What will happen to your mortal body? (verses 53–54)

h. What do you most look forward to with regard to your new, imperishable body?

DID YOU KNOW?

The next time you are in a cemetery, especially an older one, see how many of the graves are oriented in an East-West direction—with the foot of the grave pointing to the east. It was customary in cemeteries, especially those associated with a church, for the graves to face the east. This was because of the ancient tradition that said when the Lord returns to establish His kingdom He will enter through the Eastern Gate across the Kidron Valley from the Mount of Olives in Jerusalem. This was the gate through which Ezekiel saw the glory of the Lord depart (Ezekiel 10:18–19) and prophetically return (Ezekiel 43:4), and through which Jesus likely entered Jerusalem at His "triumphal entry."

Turning Point Resources
By Dr. David Jeremiah

Escape the Coming Night
In this four volume series, Dr. David Jeremiah offers a fresh, biblically sound explanation of the signs, symbols, prophecies, and omens of the end times. *Escape the Coming Night* is a penetrating look at the prophetic time machine that is the Book of Revelation—a vivid reminder of how, in the face of coming darkness, we should live today.

Soft Cover Book REVBK $13
Study Guide
  Volumes 1–4 REVSG1–4 $9 each

Cassette Tape Album	Compact Disc Album
Volume 1 REVAL1 $60	Volume 1 REVCDAL1 $84
Volume 2 REVAL2 $60	Volume 2 REVCDAL2 $84
Volume 3 REVAL3 $50	Volume 3 REVCDAL3 $70
Volume 4 REVAL4 $45	Volume 4 REVCDAL4 $63

Combined Sets Available
  Volumes 1–4, Cassette Tape Albums and Study Guides REVALSET $200
  Volumes 1–4, Compact Disc Albums and Study Guides REVCDSET $268

Tour of Duty
Marching Orders for Today's Christian Soldier

Are you on the front lines of your faith or are you MIA (missing in action)? Are you following orders or have you gone AWOL? It's not too late to be all God wants you to be! *Tour of Duty* provides the direction you need to do the Master's business while you wait for His return. A field manual for the Christian soldier, this 32-page booklet outlines 10 specific marching orders God has given every Christian. What can you be doing right now for the kingdom of God? Receive your commission and the practical instruction to fulfill it in *Tour of Duty*.

Fellowship, humility, love, unity, evangelism, obedience, righteousness . . . *Tour of Duty* is a call to action for every Christian!

Booklet TODBL $4

ORDER 1-800-947-1993

Turning Point
Resources
By Dr. David Jeremiah

Prophetic Turning Points
In an easy-to-read, question and answer format, Dr. Jeremiah presents answers to some of the most puzzling and often debated questions about Bible prophecy.

Whether you are a prophecy scholar or opening the pages of God's Word for the first time, *Prophetic Turning Points* will be a welcomed companion as you negotiate the Bible's discussion of end times. More than a helpful resource, this handbook will enable you to determine your position on life and death issues of the Christian faith.

Handbook PTPBL $6.50

Signs of the Second Coming
What Jesus Said About His Return
Do you have questions about the Second Coming? Jesus' disciples, confounded by the preliminary warnings the Lord had given them asked, "When will these things be?" Jesus replied with the longest answer to any question every put to Him. In *Signs of the Second Coming*, Dr. Jeremiah teaches the meaning behind Jesus' answer in Matthew 24 and 25, known as the Olivet Discourse.

Study Guide SSCSG $9
Cassette Album (12 tapes) SSCAL $60

ORDER 1-800-947-1993

Turning Point Resources

STUDY GUIDES

All Study Guides are regularly priced at $9
An audiocassette album is also available for each of the following series.
(Sold separately. Individually priced.)

Bend in the Road, A (Psalms)
Celebrate His Love (Christmas)
Christians Have Stress Too
Christ's Death and Resurrection
Core Values of the Church
  (I Corinthians, 3 Volumes)
Escape the Coming Night
  (Revelation, 4 Volumes)
Facing the Giants in Your Life
For Such a Time as This (Esther)
Fruit of the Spirit, The (Galatians)
Gifts from God (Parenting)
Giving to God
God in You (The Holy Spirit)
God Meant It for Good (Joseph, 2 Volumes)
Greatest Stories Ever Told, The (Parables)
Handwriting on the Wall (Daniel, 3 Volumes)
Heroes of the Faith (Hebrews)
Home Improvement
How to Be Happy According to Jesus
  (The Beatitudes)
How to Live According to Jesus
  (The Sermon on the Mount, 2 Volumes)
Invasion of Other Gods (New Age)
Investing for Eternity
Issues of the Home and Family

Jesus' Final Warning (Prophecy)
Knowing the God You Worship
Living by Faith (Romans, 3 Volumes)
Looking for the Savior (Thessalonians, 2 Volumes)
Nation in Crisis, A (Joshua, 2 Volumes)
Overcoming Loneliness
People God Uses, The
People Who Met Jesus
Power of Encouragement, The
Power of Love, The
Powerful Principles from Proverbs
Prayer—The Great Adventure
Runaway Prophet—Jonah, The
Ruth, Romance, and Redemption
Seeking Wisdom—Finding Gold
Signs of the Second Coming
Spiritual Warfare
Stewardship Is Lordship
Ten Burning Questions from Psalms
Tender Warrior, The (David, 2 Volumes)
Turning Toward Integrity (James)
Turning Toward Joy (Philippians)
What the Bible Says About Angels
When Wisdom Turns to Foolishness (Solomon)
Worship

BOOKS

Bend in the Road, A (Psalms) $19
Escape the Coming Night (Revelation) $13
Gifts from God (Parenting) $19
God in You (The Holy Spirit) $19
Handwriting on the Wall, The (Daniel) $12
Invasion of Other Gods (New Age) $13
Jesus' Final Warning (Prophecy) $19

Power of Encouragement, The $13
Prayer—The Great Adventure $19
Slaying the Giants in Your Life $19
Stories of Hope from a Bend in the Road $13
Turning Toward Integrity (James) $10
Turning Toward Joy (Philippians) $10
What the Bible Says About Angels $13

PORTABLE BOOKS

All portable books are $6

Hearing the Master's Voice (Highlights from
  Jesus' Final Warning)
Love in Action (Highlights from
  The Power of Encouragement)
Pathways of Prayer (Highlights from
  Prayer—The Great Adventure)
Priceless Gifts (Highlights from
  Gifts from God)
Truth About Angels, The (Highlights from
  What the Bible Says about Angels)
Truth About the New Age, The (Highlights from
  Invasion of Other Gods)
What If He Is Who He Says He Is? (Highlights
  from Escape the Coming Night)

BOOKLETS

Family Turning Points $6.50
Financial Turning Points $6.50
How to Encourage Your Children $2.50
Knowing God by Name $2.50
Personally Responsible to God $2.50
Powerful Prayer Promises $2.50
Prophetic Turning Points $6.50
Signs at the Bend in the Road $2.50
Tour of Duty $4.00
Walking Down the Romans Road $2.50
Who I Am in Christ $2.50
Worship $2.50
Your Greatest Turning Point $2.50

POSTAGE AND HANDLING CHART

For orders	Add
Up to $5.99	$1.50
$6.00-$19.99	$2.50
$20.00-$50.99	$3.50
$51.00-$99.99	$6.00
$100.00 & over	$9.00

If you would like a complete catalog
of resources available from
Turning Point, please call
1-800-947-1993 or write
Turning Point ~ P.O. Box 3838 ~
San Diego, CA 92163-1838.
You can also visit Turning Point at
www.turningpointonline.org